EIGHT WAYS TO BECOME CHRISTIAN

SHARING YOUR STORY OF FAITH

Douglas E. Wingeier

DISCIPLESHIP RESOURCES
MATERIALS FOR GROWTH IN CHRISTIAN FAITH AND LIFE
P.O. Box 189 • Nashville, TN 37202 • Phone (615) 340-7285

TO

The forty-four laypersons whose willingness to
share their faith stories with me has strengthened
my faith and challenged me to grow in Christian
discipleship.

ISBN 0-88177-060-4

Library of Congress Catalog Card Number: 88-71771

DR060B

CONTENTS

CHAPTER ONE

SHARING FAITH STORIES

How have you become Christian?

Close your eyes and think back over your life's journey. What have been its turning points? How have you felt the guidance of the Spirit? When and how have you met Christ along the way? What influences have shaped you? What have been the marker events that have led you into a deeper relationship with God? How have your understandings of the Christian faith changed? How have you come to live out your commitment to Christian discipleship? How have you shared your faith with those around you?

The purpose of this book is to help you reflect on these questions in light of the experience of other lay Christians, and to gain confidence and skill in sharing your faith story with others. Perhaps you have been asked to share your spiritual autobiography with a group of persons. The stories of faith told here will give you a series of windows through which to view the ways other persons have become Christian. These windows will then become mirrors as you compare your experience with theirs, and come to a clearer perception and affirmation of the ways God has been working in your life to lead you to deeper faith and discipleship. The way that others describe their faith journeys will help you appreciate and understand better how you have been opened to and have grown in your Christian experience. Their stories will also give you clues as to how you can make your journey known to others.

This book was prepared after interviews with lay Christians in three cultural settings. They were asked about their religious journeys and lives of discipleship. In the Midwest and South of mainland United States, twenty churches of four denominations (United Methodist, Presbyterian, Missouri Synod Lutheran, and Primitive Baptist) were

1

visited. In each case the pastor was asked to select a church member who was an active, committed Christian and articulate and insightful in talking about his or her faith. Then one to two hours were spent interviewing each of the persons so identified (twenty-two in all), asking them two basic questions: How have you become Christian? and, How has the church helped you in your faith journey, or, How do you wish it had?

In Hawaii a similar procedure was followed. There all but one of the persons interviewed were United Methodist. (The exception was a Quaker.) The fifteen persons came from a variety of ethnic backgrounds—Japanese, Chinese, Korean, Filipino, and Tongan, as well as Caucasian. In Australia and New Zealand, the third setting, seven persons were interviewed—five Methodists and two Presbyterians. Five were Caucasian and two were Chinese immigrants from Southeast Asia.

The faith experiences of these forty-four persons were then analyzed into categories. A total of eight pathways for becoming Christian were identified—four primarily individual in nature and the other four of a more corporate orientation. Of the twenty-six persons who described their faith experience in mainly individual terms, ten described a faith awakened through crisis or turmoil, seven spoke of a faith evoked by a significant relationship, five were experiencing a gradual maturing in faith, and four were engaged in a religious quest. The eighteen whose faith journeys were more communal in nature were divided in terms of a stable, steady life of discipleship (7), response to the challenge of service and social action (4), faith fostered in small intentional groups (4), and faith nurtured and sustained in the larger faith community (3).

Definitions

Several assumptions are basic to this book. First, faith is understood to be an attitude or relationship with God of trust, commitment, and growing understanding. Second, discipleship is viewed as lived faith (ministry) in response to a vision of what God intends for persons and the world, and in accountability to the community of faith, the Christian church. Third, the aim of ministry is seen to be the enabling of persons in community to grow in faith and discipleship and to live out the image of God through witness and service. Fourth, discipleship involves learning, living, and sharing the Christian story in both church and world. And finally, the process of "becoming Christian" is both abrupt and gradual, with sudden awakenings or transformations alternating with periods of slow, steady growth.

One clear conclusion from these stories is that "God works in mysterious ways, divine wonders to perform." The persons interviewed often spoke of events and transitions in their lives with a sense of awe and gratitude for what God had done. At the time it may have seemed like an ordinary happening, but in retrospect they became aware that God was in it, and that a pattern or plan was unfolding that had a purpose higher than their own. It is also apparent that God works in diverse ways with different people. Each person's experience was different; the Spirit's strategy varied with the need and circumstances of the individual's life.

The stories are useful, not only for the light they throw on our individual pathways but also for the insights they bring to ministries that foster faith and commitment, and to the process of sharing faith stories. Whether you are a pastor, teacher in your church, youth leader, Christian education director, evangelism coordinator, or have none of these responsibilities, you will find that these persons will teach you, as they have me, how to better focus your ministry of sharing your faith and helping others grow in faith and discipleship. Their responses to the second interview question, as well as their account of experiences in the church, give us guidance on what is needed to make our teaching more invitational, our pastoral care more sensitive to faith issues and resources, our witness more personal and meaningful, and our programming more oriented toward enabling persons to develop their identity as Christian disciples. The faith-focused ministries which these persons found most helpful or needed are in three categories: personal relationships, church plans and programs, and congregational outreach into the community.

The stories convey a powerful impression of the working of the Holy Spirit in the lives of very ordinary people. We have all been inspired by stories of heroes and heroines of the faith in times past—Moses, Ruth, Peter, Mary, Polycarp, Martin Luther, Florence Nightingale, Sojourner Truth, Toyohiko Kagawa, Albert Schweitzer, Martin Luther King, Jr., Mother Teresa, and many others. These well-known persons have lived lives of deep faith and committed discipleship which have served as example and motivation to many others to "give of their best to the Master."

But this book is about some unsung heroes and heroines of the faith—unknown people in typical churches living more or less routine lives—who nevertheless have opened their hearts to God and responded to the call of Christ in faithful, though diverse ways. Their stories reveal how they have been led into a growing understanding of the meaning and implications of their faith, a deeper commitment to embody it in their lives, and a stronger resolve to be present for others around them in the name of Christ. As such they give us encouragement. God does indeed work wonders in the lives of ordinary people like us. Our stories are indeed important and worth sharing. Our efforts as teachers and lay workers in the church can indeed have eternal significance in enabling the Spirit of God to work in the lives of others to bring about new birth and growth in faith.

The experiences described in this book are remarkable, both because they are so authentic and representative of the lives of many faithful people in our churches, and also because they offer living proof that such depth of faith, spiritual growth, and positive witness are available to any of us through Jesus Christ.

The persons described here are far from perfect. They were very honest in telling me the problems and inadequacies in their Christian lives. They are still growing, seeking, struggling. But this is what makes their stories so winsome and appealing. These are real people living everyday lives in churches and communities just like yours and mine. They haven't seen visions or been called to serve in Africa or died a martyr's death. But they strive to be faithful, nevertheless, and their stories—because they are so similar to ours—offer a compelling testimony to the power of God in Christ Jesus to transform and guide each of us into a life of purpose, risk, service, and joy in Christian discipleship.

The book begins by profiling the eight ways persons become Christian, describing the key characteristics of each pathway (Chapter Two). This is followed in Chapter Three by eight stories of faith, one representing each of the eight types of faith journey. Chapter Four then discusses the forms of ministry revealed by the study to be likely to foster faith and commitment. A final chapter draws conclusions for individual cultivation of faith and sharing of faith journeys, and offers suggestions for churches wishing to give priority to a faith-oriented plan of ministry. Questions for thought and discussion appear at the end of each chapter to assist both individual readers and study groups in exploring implications for personal faith cultivation and congregational planning.

As you prepare to explore the issues raised in this book, reflect on the following:

(1) How have I become Christian?

(2) What influences and events have been most significant in shaping my growth in faith and discipleship?

(3) How do my life and witness affect the faith journey of those about me?

(4) How does our church's program contribute to the Christian experience of persons in our congregation and community?

(5) What changes are needed in my life, and in the life of our church, to give priority to the fostering of faith and discipleship?

(6) How can I become more confident and adept at sharing my faith story with others?

CHAPTER TWO

WAYS PERSONS BECOME CHRISTIAN: EIGHT PATHWAYS

Becoming Christian is a lifelong process. The life of faith for the Christian begins with birth and baptism and continues through a series of experiences, unique to each individual, that last a lifetime. Without exception, the persons in this book trace the roots of their faith back to early childhood experiences—whether or not they were raised in Christian homes, and whether or not they underwent a sudden conversion experience at some point later in their lives.

Therefore, the phrase *becoming Christian* here refers to a process of growth that may or may not include an experience of conversion or radical change, but is also marked by periods of stability, slow steady development, and gradual transformations of understandings, attitudes, perceptions, and behavior.

Having thus identified the common element in our stories of faith— lifelong journey—let us now turn to examine the different patterns which these journeys take. What are the various ways by which persons become Christian?

Some persons speak of their faith in terms of their personal relationship with God. They think of faith primarily in individual terms. Whether sudden or gradual, their experience with Christ is inner, spiritual, relational, and characterized by a varied balance of the emotional and the intellectual. Other persons think more in terms of their relationship to the church in describing their faith journeys. They have either grown up in the church, felt accepted and challenged by the church, found avenues for service and witness through the church, or see themselves as Christian because of their involvement in the church.

A. Individual Journeys

1. AWAKENED THROUGH CRISIS OR TURMOIL

Ten of the persons interviewed—the largest number in any of the categories—experienced an awakening of their faith through facing a life crisis that led them into a period of emotional stress and unrest.

A Japanese-American woman in Hawaii became distraught over a wayward teenage son. In a church Bible study, the insight that the covenant God loved and forgave the rebellious children of Israel changed her attitude toward her son. Their relationship began to heal as she trusted God for strength and wisdom to stop criticizing her son and accept him as he was. Gradually, other areas of her life were also affected by this newfound faith and inner serenity.

A young housewife in a rural community described how she had become pregnant as a teenager, and was judged by her parents for this moral lapse. Through this experience of shame and ostracism, she and her boyfriend were driven to seek forgiveness and guidance for their lives. The result was that they began their married life together with a firm commitment to family prayer and regular church attendance, and have continued as faithful Christians ever since.

Another young woman recounted a series of trials which both tested and deepened her faith: the premature death of her mother; an early marriage, now struggling; two miscarriages; the recent death of her father; problems in their trucking business; the stroke of her father-in-law; and an unsupportive pastor. But she found a personal relationship with Christ through a charismatic group in the community, and this newfound faith was sustaining her through all of this.

A man of 78 pointed to the time years ago when his five-year-old son had been given up for dead as the crucial turning point of his life. He and his wife had prayed at the boy's bedside, and from that moment he had begun to get well. Out of gratitude to God, the man went to a tent meeting, got saved, and felt the witness of the Spirit while driving his truck a few days later. He stopped swearing, does not farm on Sundays, has become an active churchman and lay speaker, and continues to this day to read his Bible and pray daily.

A mother became upset when her son got into drugs, and called a meeting in her home of parents facing similar problems. The consultant who came had been cured of his drug problem through accepting Jesus Christ. His question to the group, "Have you tried God?" haunted this woman until she made a commitment to return to the faith and church of her youth. Now a widow of 49, her face radiated a quiet peace as she described how her faith had sustained her through a marital separation and reconciliation, and then her husband's premature death. She now shares her faith with fellow office workers, and prays each day while driving to work.

"I surrendered to the Lord when my husband left me," was the way a silver-haired woman in her late seventies described her crisis experience. She had been converted in a revival as a teenager, but had become rather lax in her faith until her troubled marriage was finally dissolved. She had believed that divorce was wrong, but through much prayer finally came to an inner resolution that allowed her to let her husband go. Since then, she has been through two auto accidents, the sudden death of her second husband, and the heartbreak caused by the divorce of her middle-aged son—finding strength to bear all of this in a personal relationship with God that she traces back to the surrender she made at the time of her divorce.

An active churchwoman in her later years had her faith tested and deepened through a conflict with her pastor. She blamed him for their estrangement, and harbored a grudge in her heart for several years. This resentment kept eating at her until finally she screwed up her courage to confront him. They had it out, were reconciled, and then prayed together. The relief and healing that took place in her heart at that moment led her to a deeper walk with God which has since led to her receiving the baptism of the Holy Spirit and the gift of tongues. She reports being healed of a near-fatal ailment, and is active in both the women's society of her local church and a nondenominational charismatic Bible study group in her community.

Loneliness, family stress, guilt, the illness or death of a loved one, divorce, a personal conflict—such crises, and the inner turmoil they produce, pave the way for an awakened and deepened experience of faith. Persons are challenged to open their lives, accept Christ and receive the Spirit, seek forgiveness and reconciliation, find new direction for their lives, and are launched into new depths of faith and wider paths of service through the impulse of such experiences.

2. FAITH EVOKED BY A SIGNIFICANT RELATIONSHIP

Seven persons traced the origin of their quickened faith back to an important relationship with a person who had exercised a profound influence on their lives.

The key figure in the turn to faith of one young man was his theology teacher in the Jesuit high school to which his parents had sent him. For him, the young priest embodied "what a Christian would be like"—full of joy and fun, interested in theology and able to make it stimulating, and genuinely concerned about him as a person. The boy was fully accepted as a Protestant. His questions and ideas were taken seriously, and the complete absence of pressure to convert him made him responsive to the symbolism of the Mass, the invitation to prayer, and the opening up of his mind to the challenge of Christian commitment. He had been brought up in loose association with Baptist revivalism and eventually found his home in a Missouri Synod Lutheran Church. But it was this prolonged encounter with an authentic Christian in the person of a Roman Catholic priest who became his counselor and friend that really led him to make a personal commitment to Jesus Christ.

It was one man's 12-year-old daughter who turned him from a life of alcoholism to give his heart to Christ and become active in the church. Converted at age 15 in a Baptist revival, this man began drinking in the military and was a slave to alcohol for many years. One night at the kitchen table his daughter confronted him: "Daddy, the one thing you can't do is let the bottle alone, and I'm afraid it's going to kill you. I don't think you can stop unless God will make you stop." That was the challenge he needed; he quit drinking at that point, and has resisted it ever since. He returned to the church, began teaching Sunday school, does lay speaking, and today is a pillar in his Southern Presbyterian Church.

Another man's experience was similar. He was not brought up in the church, and went to the Lutheran Church with his wife and children only on Christmas and Easter. One by one, as his children were confirmed, they asked him, "Daddy, when are you going to get involved in the church?" His stock reply was, "One of these times." Finally, at the age of 50, when his youngest daughter received this answer, she said, "Shouldn't 'one of these times' be right now?" Shaken up by this direct confrontation, the man could only respond, "Yes, the next time the pastor offers a class for adults, I'll go." True to his word, he took the class, joined the church, became active, and his life has been changing ever since. He has given up Sunday sports in order to be in church. He has learned to rely on God in facing struggles such as the decision to put his father in a nursing home, and the divorces of his two daughters. He has overcome his childhood prejudices toward minority races through the influence of the gospel. And in recent times he has been a mainstay of his pastor and congregation as they went through a difficult financial crisis.

For a young Japanese man in Hawaii, it was his fiancée's ultimatum that started him on the path to Christian commitment. In response to a marriage proposal she asked, "If I agree to marry you, will you promise to attend church every Sunday?" He had been raised as a staunch Buddhist, but his love for her led him to accept Christianity and gradually become active in the church. The later ten-year ministry of an influential pastor helped them both "understand God's love and grow strong spiritually in Christian discipleship and stewardship." Today, at 69, he is a leading layman in Hawaiian Methodism, and in retirement gives much time and energy to both local and denominational church activities.

The example of a Christ-like teacher and model, the steadfast love and trust of a husband, the confrontation and challenge of children, the invitation of a loved one to join in a lifelong journey of companionship and faith—these are only illustrative of the impact another person can have in calling one to follow Christ. Whether a deliberately planned summons or an unconscious influence, the witness of Christian disciples, young and old, can have a powerful effect in leading persons along in the journey of faith and discipleship.

3. GRADUAL MATURING IN FAITH

For five persons interviewed, their faith seems simply to unfold like a flower as they develop and mature. One, a retired farmer, recalled a lifetime of living in the same small community and attending the same church with faithful regularity. Certain high points stood out, such as a revival led by a colorful evangelist when he was thirteen, raising money to pay for the church windows, being fascinated by Old Testament stories and maps of Bible lands, joining the church at the same time as his father and brothers, the merger of Presbyterian and Methodist congregations, the premature death of a beloved sister which was eased by both her strong faith and his, and three years of near-total crop failure which made him realize that "maybe there's more to life than piling up land and crops," and that "God will see you through." Today, at 71, he expresses a thoughtful concern for the hungry of the world, soil conservation and the care of the earth, the farm crisis, drug abuse, and other contemporary problems—all in the context of a biblical faith and global perspective. Wisdom and insight have come to this man out of a lifetime of worship and study in a small rural church.

Somewhat more dramatic, but nevertheless gradual and steady, has been the spiritual development of a 56-year-old retired teacher. His growth in faith, though, has been punctuated by several turning points, including a hang glider accident that left him lying on his back with much time to reflect, rejection for a church office he coveted, and a work mission in Haiti. He views his recent retirement as a "commencement" for the next phase of his life, the nature of which is still undetermined. A lifetime of church attendance and varying degrees of activity was now culminating in deeper spiritual dedication, characterized by daily devotions and a sense that "I am a new person; I've had a rebirth of the spirit." He is reading the Bible more, and claims a constant awareness of Jesus' presence. He states, "The more you know Jesus, the more you love him; and the more you love him, the more you want to do for him. I feel that I'm maturing, though still in my childhood as far as Christian knowledge is concerned." This man is now contemplating ways of becoming more involved in Christian work in his retirement—possibly through leading more work missions in the Caribbean.

The only Quaker interviewed was the wife of a retired university professor. She had spent her life in the Friends community, and exhibited a serenity, sparkle, and zest for life that were contagious. She had been nurtured in an appreciation for the inner witness, respect for all persons, willing service, and prophetic action for peace and justice. She and her husband had taught in a black college, lived in a black neighborhood, marched in demonstrations, taken risks for unpopular causes, and most recently coordinated Quaker work in Honolulu in their retirement. Her life had been a firm, undeviating response to the leading of the inner Light.

Slow, steady growth in faith and discipleship is one common pattern among Christians in today's church. Their journeys are perceived as individual, but are nurtured in the community of faith, through opportunities for renewed commitment, study and broadened understanding, and outreach through service and witness.

4. ENGAGED IN A RELIGIOUS QUEST

Four of the persons interviewed had faith journeys best characterized in terms of a religious quest. One young woman, for example, though raised in an atheistic home, from early childhood was always probing the spiritual dimensions of life. Left free to think and choose for herself, she pursued her "search for answers" in her parents' Unitarian church, a secular Jewish Sunday school, religious movies and books, association with evangelical Christian friends in high school and college, and finally in a small women's prayer group and the life of a United Methodist church in a university town. Soon after she started attending, she took the membership class, was baptized, and united with this church, and has since been eagerly soaking up Christian nurture through worship services, study groups, Sunday school teaching, and her own avid reading. Her faith is growing deeper and stronger as she moves beyond the basics to grapple with profound questions, engage in a life of discipleship, and think about the spiritual nurture of her two-year-old son.

Another example of religious quest is an eighteen-year-old high school graduate who enjoys having fun, but also ponders the meaning of life. As a Korean-American, he experiences the usual tension between his values and goals and those of the older generation who migrated to America from Korea. He speaks of the abnormally high suicide rate among his high school peers—young people who just found it too difficult to cope with the parental pressures, racial discrimination, and drug abuse and moral laxity of their adopted culture. He has found a home and sense of direction in the English congregation of his Korean church, and has identified with the youth fellowship and young pastor there. He speaks with hope and enthusiasm about the future, but still has lots of questions. He wonders why the Korean congregation of his elders has to be so conservative and unsympathetic to the needs of young people. He asks about death, commitment, service, and the divinity of Christ. His quest has led him to accept Christ as Savior and to join the church, but he still questions some of the church teachings and practices he has encountered. He has embarked on a lifelong quest of faith.

Whether it begins early or late in life, some persons seem to have a driving thirst to experience God, understand the faith, and probe the meaning and purpose of life. They take the initiative in raising questions, seeking answers, and finding satisfaction for their spiritual urges.

B. Formed in Community

1. A STABLE, STEADY LIFE OF DISCIPLESHIP

A fifth pattern of growth in faith, identified in six of the persons interviewed, is one of continuous, dependable participation and service in and through the church.

One woman grew up in a Christian home and church in rural Oklahoma, found revivals "scary," and did not really develop a firm faith until she and her husband joined a friendly, caring church in the city. Going to church and Sunday school was a way of life for her as a child, but it was only in some treasured times with her grandfather that she really felt the presence of God. She looks back on a gallery of heroes and heroines in the faith—strong Christians who were influences for good in the community and set an example for her to follow. The Wesley Foundation provided a nurturing environment in college, and it was there she met her husband. They moved a lot during the early years of his career, and she felt shy and lonely, did not really get involved in a church though she tried, and lost a baby in childbirth which was a challenge to her faith. Finally finding a church home, she grew into a skilled and dedicated church school teacher, becoming a certified lab leader. Through this ministry of Christian education as well as active leadership in the P.T.A., she matured as a person and a Christian, developed self-confidence, and became a committed, respected church leader. Hers is not a flamboyant witness, but rather a quiet, steady, radiant faith that inspires confidence and trust. It has sustained her through church conflicts, serious illness, the unexpected loss of her father, and struggles with a rebellious teenage daughter.

A Georgia mother described herself as "the churchiest person in my family." Her parents attended church, but were not leaders. They had a blessing at mealtimes and discussed religion at the table. She never missed Sunday school, started youth fellowship before she was old enough, became a district and conference officer, and had a mountaintop experience at church camp, where she made a commitment to "full-time Christian service"—several times. She majored in Christian education and took a church job after graduation, which she held until her marriage. She has a searching faith, is well read theologically, and has become a stimulating teacher of the young couples' class in her local church. She is optimistic, energetic, a pillar of strength to others, and still enjoys her intellectual freedom and curiosity. Her faith has sustained her through the death of her father, illnesses of her children, and the ups and downs of pastoral changes not all to her liking. It provides the motivating power for continued lay volunteer service in church and community, and an engaging witness which commends her faith and her Lord to those about her.

Another example of stable discipleship is a retired school superintendent who shows up every day at his church to help manage the building, supervise maintenance, and help however he is needed. A lifetime of active churchmanship in a number of congregations is now being capped by nearly fulltime voluntary service. This man finds fulfillment and challenge through giving his time in this way, and sees it as just another expression of the Christian faith and discipleship that has characterized most of his adult life.

After Sunday school influence as a child and a period of activity in a young adult group while in college, a Chinese-American doctor spent seventeen years away from the church. This was due partly to disappointment with a lazy pastor, and partly to his moving away from the community where he held church membership. It was only three years ago that he came back into the church, but since then he has become a choir member, deacon, and active church supporter. He sees church membership as a civic responsibility, and participates in worship as a stimulus to honest, dependable Christian practices. His renewed faith has enabled him to move out of a severe emotional depression, and to gain a new sense of confidence through "a strong relationship with God." His service to the community, desire to help other people, and faithful leadership in the church, are all motivated by his religious faith. His is a journeyman's faith. It is neither very articulate nor very outgoing. But it is stable and steady, to be depended upon.

Another man describes himself as a "stable, steady provider in the church," and it is his language that is used to describe this category. He "was born into the church," brought up a Methodist, and had a positive experience in Epworth League camps. He says he was born again at age fifteen in a Four-Square church in California, but "didn't change all that much simply because I already was practicing . . . ; I've just gone right on." He has been an active leader in the church all his life. Widely traveled and well read, he currently serves as civilian regional director of education for the Air Force, a post through which he gives active expression to his faith. He experiences God as a liberating "personal force" in his life, holds a "fundamental belief in God and in Christ" that is "the way to go," and attends church as "my place to worship God, as part of my due, part of life." His faith suffered a rude shock and consequent deepening and maturing a few years ago when he made a major decision in response to what he believed to be the will of God, and "it turned out I was completely wrong and it shook me quite a bit for awhile. Since then, it has been kind of a coming back again and rethinking what is God." He has not lost his faith, but is simply rethinking it, and his participation in the church is as stable and steady as ever. He respects people of other faiths, is concerned about issues of world peace and racial equality, strives to be open and honest in administering his program, and objects to an aggressive, manipulative approach to evangelism. Humbly, he says, I'm just "trying to be a Christian."

Stable, steady discipleship through active leadership in the church and deliberate effort to be honest and responsible in all aspects of life, is a common pattern of Christian faith in the mainline churches. Such persons may not be vibrant and eloquent witnesses, but they are the backbone of the church and of responsible, moral leadership in the world.

2. THE CHALLENGE OF SERVICE AND SOCIAL ACTION

Five persons identified Christian service and social concern as central to their growth in faith. One man, at age seventy, is now embarking on his third career—all service-oriented, and motivated by his Christian faith. He has spent his entire life in one small rural church, within easy driving distance of a large Midwestern university. He went forward and confessed his faith in Christ during a church revival when he was eleven, and his faith was challenged and solidified by several years of Epworth League summer camp during his adolescence. Always a sensitive boy, he recalls viewing the enemy during his war service as human beings and not as beasts as they were portrayed by military propaganda. Returning from the war, he became a university personnel officer and operated a student rooming house out of a concern to serve the needs of college students. When his parents passed away, he resigned his university position, took training as a practical nurse, helped to found a nursing home in his community, and worked there for several years serving the needs of aging patients. Recently, he has left that work and gone to Haiti to learn Creole and start a third career working with the Methodist Church there. While this man does not express his faith in religious language, and does not claim a regular prayer life, his concern for human need and dedication to service has made him a living witness through active discipleship.

One of the oldest men interviewed was one who, in his later years and out of his faith commitment, had become an advocate for gay rights. Raised an orthodox Presbyterian, he was opened up to a more tolerant, accepting attitude through a formative comparative religion course in college. Consistently interested in the scholarly side of the Christian faith, and always something of a rebel, he had done serious study of theology and church history, questioned traditional dogma such as predestination, and drove a car carrying bumper stickers that read "Question Authority" and "The Moral Majority Is Neither." At age sixty, with three children and four grandchildren, he "came out" and acknowledged his own homosexual orientation. Since then he has waged a tireless campaign, both in society at large and within The United Methodist Church, to win recognition for the civil and human rights of the gay community. This man was never a practicing homosexual and remains married to this day, but believes that "God was driving me to be more honest" and acknowledge his homosexuality, and that God continues to lead him today to work actively for the well-being of the gay people with whom he has identified. His faith leads him to an optimistic view of the future for this cause, causing him to assert that "the Creator God is going to bring about greater acceptance of gays as normal human beings, and thereby make us what I call better Christians."

Social activism, though on different issues, is likewise the lifeblood of the faith of one of the women interviewed. Divorced and remarried, she has been energized by the women's movement. Her raised consciousness as a woman has developed hand in glove with a renewed and focused Christian faith. A nominal Christian and practicing Episcopalian for most of her adult life, her marriage to an active Methodist layman brought about a shift into The United Methodist Church, where she found a concern for women's issues and some theological and human support for her emerging identity as a strong woman of faith. Her commitment to justice for women has broadened to active concern for the environment and the cause of peace and nuclear disarmament. At times she gets discouraged at the slowness of other church people to see the implications of their faith for these issues, but she is at the same time sustained and challenged to deeper commitment and bolder action by other segments of the same church.

Whether the challenge is to service in response to human need or prophetic action for peace, justice, and human rights, the Christian faith is clearly related to social needs and issues in the eyes of these persons and others whom they represent. A life committed to Christian service and social action is one of the principal pathways to deepened faith and discipleship discovered in this study.

3. INVOLVEMENT IN SMALL INTENTIONAL GROUPS

Another avenue for becoming Christian is participation in small, nurturing groups, both within and beyond the church. "My life has been the church," says one woman who, in recent years, has found a deeper walk with Christ and the baptism of the Holy Spirit through involvement in the nondenominational, charismatic Christian Women's Club in her community. She has also started a prayer group in her own church to extend the small group ministry and invite other persons into a deeper experience with God. Lured into the Christian Women's Club through the witness of four women who "had something that I lacked and wanted," she found a deep joy and peace, received the gift of tongues, and has developed a serenity and compassion that cause other people to come to her with their problems. Now sixty-two, she has held every office imaginable in the church, but is currently devoting her energy primarily to prayer, Bible study, personal counseling, and witnessing through these small, intimate spiritual groups. Such experiences both nourish her own faith and give her opportunity to practice discipleship by leading others into a deeper relationship with the Lord.

Perhaps the most unique, colorful story in the entire study is that of a 39-year-old divorcée whose faith journey encompasses a wide variety of spiritual experiences, but whose life in recent years has been redirected and stabilized through participating in the Cursillo movement in the Episcopal Church. Early religious influences included baptism at three months, an emotional conversion precipitated by reading a biography of the Virgin Mary at age ten, attending a Mormon Church as a teenager, and exposure to a variety of faiths through a college world religions class. In the 1960s she got involved in the youth drug culture. Taking LSD "for me was, at times, a very strong spiritual experience." She joined a hippie commune, got very sick, and during her long recuperation from serious surgery began to meditate through use of Hindu mantras. Living with an alcoholic led her into Alanon, where she had another spiritual awakening. "In forgiving I was healed myself," she said, and started to "straighten up my life a lot." As a local newspaper reporter, she covered an Assembly of God revival led by a woman faith healer, and through this was moved to embark on a serious reading of the New Testament. This led to joining a conservative Episcopal Church, where the liturgy appealed to her. Here she got involved with Cursillo, which influenced her to draw up "an apostolic plan" for her own ministry to Christianize her environment. She also follows their daily prayer discipline, and attends the weekly meeting of her "reunion group" for prayer and personal support. This challenges her to put her faith into action through her job as a journalist, and offers guidance for public action on issues such as child abuse and personal decisions in areas such as sexuality and the raising of her two teenage daughters. Summing up her multi-faceted faith journey, this remarkable woman says, "Much of my life has been destructive and wasteful, but each thing has brought me to another level of spiritual growth. It's just amazing. You never know what God is going to do. It gives you a lot of faith in the fact that you will be led, that you can trust and relax. I'm continually growing in that, and I'm going on to perfection."

4. NURTURED AND SUSTAINED IN THE FAITH COMMUNITY

Faith grows in some people from seeds planted in the fertile soil of a faithful, caring congregation. Three persons of this type were interviewed. One was a 45-year-old divorcée with two teenage children who recited a string of significant church-related experiences that marked her growth in faith up to that point in her life. "I became a Christian because of an evolutionary process," she said. Baptized in her first year and raised in a Christian home, she accepted Christ as personal Savior as a first-grader, through the influence of a woman dear to her who had a "real and vital relationship with Christ." She learned the Lord's Prayer, Apostles' Creed, and stories of the Bible, in the course of her regular Sunday school participation, and felt nourished by the church throughout her childhood and youth. "Confirmation was special," and a closing night Communion at church camp brought renewed commitment as a young person. Teaching Sunday school in high school gave her a sense of ability and worth. And the church community provided support during several years of troubled marriage which led to a suicide attempt and eventual divorce. She felt God calling her to leave her husband, put her life in order, provide a more wholesome environment for her children, become a more consistent witness, and devote her life to work in the church with her high school youth. The church has been this woman's life; it has given her hope in a dark time of despondency; and now she is returning her life to the church in capable, productive ways.

A Filipina in Hawaii, who came from a long line of pastors and deaconnesses, was steeped in the tradition of active church life and discipleship. "Christianity was in me all the time, because of my background." The role models in her family, daily prayer and devotions in the home, attending Sunday school rallies and youth institutes, teaching Sunday school from an early age, memorizing Bible verses for children's contests, talking with older Christians and hearing their stories, and finally attending a church college to receive training for deaconness work—all were part of her formation process. Today she has become the kind of vital witness and stable Christian influence in the lives of others that her family had been for her. She has placed a Bible in the bathroom, where her busy family can read it. She has engaged in an outreach ministry to Filipino immigrants, seeking to draw them into her congregation. She recently suffered a mild stroke, has been sustained through that crisis by her strong faith, and was able to witness to her hospital roommate. Just as older folks had passed on their faith to her as a child, so she now is telling her story to others. "It just comes spontaneously," she says. "If it's in your heart, and if it's personal experience, then you can share more when you talk about your life. That's how I grow in faith."

Persons such as these find and grow in faith primarily through the caring, challenging influence of the local congregation. And this in turn leads them to continue the nurturing influence through their own lives of discipleship.

Eight pathways to develop faith and discipleship have been described here. Each has provided nurture and guidance to deepening commitment for some Christians. A combination of these ways in which persons become Christian would likely be represented in the diversity of members that makes up every Christian congregation.

Questions for Thought and Discussion

As you reflect on the eight pathways to faith and discipleship, consider the following questions:

1. Do you find your own pathway to becoming Christian represented here? If so, how is your story the same as or different from those described here?

2. If your experience does not fit any of these patterns, how would you characterize it?

3. How would you identify the activity of the Holy Spirit in each of the eight pathways? Reflect on the balance and interaction between God's initiative and human effort in each type of faith journey, and in your own.

4. At what points in this chapter were your own faith and disci-

pleship illuminated and/or challenged to further growth? What steps do you intend to take in your own religious pilgrimage as a result?

5. Which of these patterns do you find in the members of your congregation? How can your church program foster faith and discipleship in each of these pathways?

6. How can you encourage persons in your church to share their faith experiences with one another?

CHAPTER THREE

EIGHT STORIES OF FAITH

We have seen in the previous chapter examples and characteristics of each of the eight pathways to developing Christian faith and discipleship. Now we have an opportunity to come to know eight persons of faith more fully. We will listen and learn as one person in each of the categories tells the story of how he/she has been born and has grown in the Christian faith. As you read, watch for comparisons with your own faith journey, and also for ways in which the church fostered or could have fostered each person's growth in faith.

A. Individual Pathways

1. ANA K. KUMĀ: THE WORDS TOUCHED MY HEART

Ana Kumā, a sixteen-year-old high school senior from the South Pacific Island of Tonga, is doing her homework in an empty classroom in a downtown Honolulu church. She comes here every day because her home is so crowded and noisy that she cannot concentrate. Her father is the custodian, so she helps him with the cleaning after her school work is done.

Today, after finishing her lessons, she takes a Bible from the shelf and opens to Matthew 11, where these words jump out at her: "Come to me, all who labor and are heavy laden, and I will give you rest. Take my yoke upon you, and learn from me; . . . , and you will find rest for your souls. For my yoke is easy, and my burden is light" (verses 28-30).

"You know," says Ana, "those words really touched my heart, and it came to me that Jesus really wanted to help me. A voice inside was saying, 'God knows what you're going through and he wants to help you.' And so my desire really grew to know Jesus more."

Teenage Turmoil

Ana's life was greatly upset at this time. Her father and mother had separated while still in Tonga, and she had been brought to Hawaii as a ten-year-old by her father and grandmother. They were living in a small apartment, crowded together with other relatives.

"Life was pretty tough for me," exclaims Ana. "I was living with an extended family, and did not have my privacy, my personal time, because there were just too many people in the house. Even though we were poor, we still opened our hearts and home to them. But as the years went by, it became very difficult. I had no intimacy with my own family, because of other families interfering."

"Also, most of the time I ended up doing the work, because it was my home and I really cared about how it looked. I didn't have a mother, and that's why all this burden was upon me—'women's work,' you know. My grandmother wasn't strong enough to do the work, so I ended up being just like a housewife, while at the same time going to school and doing my homework. So I was very depressed. My home was not a very pleasant place to go back to after school."

Distraught by the pressure, turmoil, and lack of support and understanding at home, Ana sought escape in the quiet of an empty church. She was deeply troubled by the absence of love and appreciation in her life. Without really knowing it, she was longing for someone to give her the love that she would have received from her mother.

The Bible Comes to Life

Then, "one day something happened." She went to the classroom and did her homework as usual, but instead of going down to help her father, she picked up a Bible and started to read. She had learned many Bible stories and verses in Sunday school back in Tonga years ago, but had scarcely looked inside a Bible since. Now, however, something prompted her to open and read—"just to kill time," she said.

Almost immediately she became engrossed in what she was reading, and kept on. Finally, "not knowing that I had been reading for two hours, I looked at my watch and thought, 'I have to put this away and get down real fast and start working.' The next day the same thing happened. I went back to the room, and hurried to finish my homework so I could go back to reading the Bible. Every day I would come, do all my homework, put it away, and read the Bible. Each day my interest in the Bible increased, and one day the words became so alive to me, you know, so real."

In that moment, Ana felt Jesus speaking to her and offering her the comfort and acceptance she had so long been seeking. "This was the first time I ever felt God was real to me, when the Word became so alive." Ana's heart had been "strangely warmed." The light of Christ's love flowed into her heart, her burden was lifted, and she felt joy and hope again.

Childhood in Tonga

Ana Kumā had known about God and Jesus all her life. She describes her religious background in Tonga this way. "Intellectually, I always knew there was a God. My grandmother was a very religious person, and she always attended church. Every Sunday I was expected to go to Sunday school. I learned many stories in the Old and New Testaments, and memorized many verses.

"I was raised in a Methodist church. We had maybe a couple of Bible stories on Sunday morning—ten minutes before the worship began. But then again at 2:00 in the afternoon we would hear the bell, and all the children would go back to the church for Sunday school. There was also a test at the end of each year, and if you passed you moved up to the next class. The test was over Bible knowledge; that's how I came to memorize so much scripture. The examiner would call us up individually and ask us several questions out of the Bible." Unquestionably, Ana had had a solid Bible background in her Sunday school training.

Changed Attitudes

But now the Word had "touched her heart," and God was speaking to her through it. The foundation had been laid in her childhood, and now it was taking on meaning for her as she eagerly searched it daily for fresh insights into her newfound faith. "My heart really felt the presence of God in that time. I was hungry to know God more. So I began to become more active in the church. I joined the pastor's Bible study class, and I was the only young person in it, because the youth were not active at that time."

In her developing prayer life, Ana was led to turn her problems over to the Lord. "I said to God, 'Okay, I lift my problem at home to you, God. You take care of this problem, because I cannot.' God said, 'Love others as you love yourself.' But I'd say, 'There's no way I'm going to love these relatives of mine, Lord.' So I said to the Lord, 'No, I just can't—my love is selfish and I cannot love them. But then I prayed to God, 'Only through the love of Christ can I love my relatives. Change my heart, Lord, create in me a new heart!' And you know, I don't hold any grudges against my relatives any more. I look at them from a new perspective. The negative feelings are gone. I'm glad to see them come to my house now; I'm glad to help them."

Ana also had a new desire in her heart to worship God and seek God's will for her life. "So from then on God became so real and I wanted to come to church. I don't want to miss any worship. It's not a hassle any more.

"And I'm seeking God's will for me. I don't know what my call is going to be, but I'm in the process. At the age of nineteen I don't know yet. There are lots of possibilities. I just say, 'May your will be done in me, God. Just prepare me to go wherever you want me. I'll be glad to do it. I'm impatient sometimes, though. Going to school I want to know where I'm headed so I can take the right courses to prepare me. But there's no piece of paper falling from heaven telling me what my goals are to be."

Ana seems open to following God's leading, but impatient that no specific directions are yet forthcoming. At the same time, she is pursuing a day-to-day obedience in her walk with God. "It's just a matter of devotion to my daily duties, and doing what I know I'm supposed to, like loving others. I realize God is working in me and showing me my stubbornness, my self-centeredness. I have to work

just to become the person I'm supposed to be. I'm constantly changing and growing." Ana is finding the Christian life a struggle and a
challenge, but the effort is bearing fruit.

Need for a Mother

What was behind Ana'a conversion? How does she understand the
wonderful change that has come into her life? She is well aware that
it is related to her intense loneliness and longing for love. "It was
because I was always desperate to have a mother. Back in Tonga I was
living with my father and grandmother. But my mother lived only a
couple of houses away, so I could easily go visit her. But when I came
to Hawaii there were many burdens in a new environment. So I was
homesick for my mother. I used to really cry inside. When problems
got to be too much at home, I was tempted to say, 'If I only had a
mother!' But then, when God came to be real to me, I didn't say this
any more, because now I knew that God was going to help me."

God also provided a human companion, however. "I think," she
told me, "that God's way of enabling me to have a mother was
through the church. Because, you know, the church secretary has
become my best friend. I think of her as my Caucasian mother. We
have a really intimate relationship. I can complain to her and tell her
my problems. I see that God, through her, is fulfilling that empty part
of me."

God has filled the void in Ana's life which was caused by the
absence of her mother. She now has found a relationship with Christ,
and also with a substitute mother, both of whom would not only
comfort and sustain her, but also give her a changed perspective on
her situation.

Nurture by the Church

A deepening prayer life, changed attitudes, and regular participation in worship and Bible study gradually led Ana to another decision. She wanted to become a member of the church, and saw this as
a natural and necessary expression of the commitments she had
already made. "Long before I went through the ceremony, I already

was a member of the Church of Christ. Going through the membership training and standing before the congregation has given me more meaning, though, and caused me to devote more of my life to the church. I now want to reach out to other members who are not active, and share my faith with them."

Ana is also very active in the church youth and young adult groups, where she is finding a need met that was long neglected. "I was always around adults," she says, "so I missed those times of feeling like a child and acting silly. I had no free time to express myself; I always had to work and fulfill my responsibilities. But now, by being with the youth, I am learning to enjoy myself more and to relive some of my youth. It has been kind of fun."

Future Prospects and Decisions

In this young adult group Ana has met a young man named Jeffrey to whom she is now engaged. In enthusiastic tones she talks about this new love in her life: "I met my fiancé in this church. He's a Caucasian from the mainland. He was seeking help. He hated the life he was in. He was involved in drugs, and drinking a lot. He was from a pretty well-off family and had all he wanted. But he came to Hawaii to get away from that life. His background is Methodist, so when he got here he looked in the phone book, found our church, came and talked with the pastor, and got real help with his problems.

"One morning I was walking with him, and telling him about my new life, how God had become so real to me. As a result of my sharing that with him, and the pastor's counseling, he has become a different person. He's a Christian right now. It's just funny the way things work out."

With her sense of calling and desire to serve Christ in the future, and now her approaching marriage, Ana clearly will be facing some conflicts and decisions down the way. But she also has the resources to deal with them—both in her church and in her relationship with God through Christ.

Daily Nourishment

Each day before she goes to her present job as a teacher's aide in the church nursery school, Ana cultivates this relationship. "Every morning I read my Bible for thirty minutes. I don't understand it all, but I am very interested in it. And the pastor helps explain it if I have a question. I have a devotional guide, and I read it and the Bible and pray. And then during the day, if I have a five-minute break, I go upstairs to an empty classroom, and I just close the door and do my prayers. I can't start working without praying, because I will feel really weak. So I'm really depending on God every day for strength."

Ana Kumā has come a long way in the three years since Christ came into her heart. She has much to be thankful for—both in her religious upbringing in Tonga and also in her new church home where her spiritual growth has been nourished by a sensitive pastor, a supportive congregation, and a stimulating worship and study program. Now she is ready for what lies ahead. She has accepted the challenge of following Christ. She is willing to obey his leading. As she puts it, "I made that choice, I accepted God. He was knocking on the door all along, and finally I let him in. Once I made that choice, I knew I had to commit myself. I am ready to follow wherever he leads me."

Questions for Thought and Discussion

1. What factors led up to and made possible Ana's conversion experience? How do you see God working in her life through these circumstances?

2. In what ways has the church been helpful to Ana? What more might it have done?

3. What can we learn from Ana's story about approaches to ministry with (a) immigrant families, (b) poor families, and (c) children and youth in divorced families?

4. What parts of Ana's story make you glad? What gives you cause for concern?

5. What issues do you foresee Ana having to deal with in the next phase of her journey? How can the church be helpful to her as she encounters these?

6. How do you personally relate to Ana's story? How can her experience illumine and guide your faith journey? What does the way she tells it suggest about ways you might share your faith experience with others?

2. SALLY STEELE: ACCEPTED AS I AM

A Midwestern farm wife in her early thirties, Sally Steele's transformation took place in response to the love of her husband. As a teenager, she felt unaccepted, unloved, and was living her life out of a strong inner pressure to please her father. She developed anorexia nervosa and was slowly starving herself to death. But then she and Kenneth fell in love, and it was his acceptance, strength, and quiet belief in her that gradually helped her develop the self-confidence and sense of purpose to pick up her life and walk.

Childhood: A Desire to Be Good

Sally's mother took her to Sunday school, but her father didn't go. She can remember being eager to read the Bible from an early age. "My mother and father brought me up with good moral standards. I didn't do the things you shouldn't do, and I had a desire in my heart to be good. And yet I still didn't know the Lord."

Her family did not have regular grace before meals, but she remembers saying bedtime prayers. "They were prayers within myself, not initiated by my parents." "I went to Sunday school and M.Y.F.," she says, and recalls receiving attendance awards and learning stories about Daniel and Jonah. One special memory was of a couple who taught her junior high class. "They were unique, you know; their relationship was really neat. This man admired his wife and she in turn respected him; they were very open in sharing with us, and I appreciated that. They made a difference, I think."

Disillusionment in College

"The real critical times started to develop when I was sixteen going on seventeen in high school. I had an inferiority complex, and developed anorexia nervosa. That began a struggle of really being lost. I was to the point of really wanting to die. I hated myself. I was so lonely and felt so unloved. There was a lot of pressure, a lot of loneliness, a lot of lostness, not knowing who I was or what I wanted to do for sure. I didn't have anyone to just hold me and say you're okay as a person, because I didn't feel okay as a person.

Sally went off to college in this state, and things went from bad to worse. "I was thrown into a situation where I was really naive. I thought everybody was good and wonderful, but I soon found that the girls in my dorm were sleeping around with guys and that there were drugs on campus, and it just blew my little world all to pieces. Other people didn't share my moral standards. I had been living in a make-believe world. I was afraid of failing my parents. I didn't want to go to college, really, and yet I was there because I didn't want to fail my father."

"And then the Lord led into my life the man who is now my husband." Kenneth was three years older, and they had fallen in love when she was a senior in high school. He was back home, and she was away at college, lonely and confused. He was a Christian, and when she came home he told her, "If you would ask the Lord would answer, if you would knock he would open the door, and if you'd ask you would receive."

So Sally went back to the Wesley Fellowship on campus and attended a Wednesday night Communion service. "I can remember kneeling there and feeling so terrible, and the Lord Jesus was saying, 'If you just give it up I'll take it over.' I'd read the Bible but didn't understand it, yet at that point I *knew* he was Lord; I *knew* he had died for me; I *knew* he could carry all these things that were about to crush me and take my life.

"From that point on, Kenneth and I began to read *The Upper Room* and the Bible together on our dates, and I began to understand because the Lord began to explain the scriptures to me. At that point I gave my heart to him, and understood that he really came for *me*. That was the point where my life began to change, where I began to understand what Christianity was—more than just going to church and being a good person. I wanted to die physically, but I died to what I wanted, and let him come into my heart. It wasn't flashing lights; it was just that I *knew* that day at the Communion table that he came for me, and that it didn't have to be the way it was, that it could be different."

An Accepting Husband

It was the strong, silent, steadfast love of her husband-to-be that finally convinced Sally of her own self-worth. "He was finally the one that the Lord used to show me that I could be loved unconditionally. I would get hateful because I wanted people to love me, but I couldn't drive him away. He stuck with me; he was just very firm. He was always there, no matter what I did. So I thought, 'This is the guy I really want to marry.' I think that helped bring me to the Lord, the fact that he loved me no matter what. It didn't matter if I was hateful or nice, if I did the right things or the wrong things, he always loved me. He was the first person I ever came in contact with who was Christlike. He is a man of few words, but his actions are always right on the mark. When we were dating, it didn't matter if I would want to do something on Sunday, he went to church. He was dedicated, and I began to see that in a lot of areas he was different, and I appreciated that."

Kenneth was brought up by Christian parents in a home where prayer and Bible reading were an everyday occurrence. "They prayed for their children and guided them and tried to lead them in the way that they would accept the Lord. He can never remember not knowing the Lord." This stability appealed to Sally; it was just what she needed.

In response to Kenneth's accepting love and steadying influence, Sally began to grow as a person and as a Christian. They decided they wanted to get married, and that she would drop out of college. She feared that this would disappoint and anger her father, but he accepted it better than they expected. "I began to get the courage to believe that my decisions were okay—that I could pray about them and make the decisions that I thought were best for me, instead of worrying about what my Mom and Dad would think. Instead of trying to live for someone else, I began to let the Lord help me live my life the way he wanted me to live it. I began studying the Bible; I really had a desire to know God."

Growth and Struggle in the Faith

Newly married and new in the faith, Sally was fortunate in that her pastor organized a group of young couples in their church for Bible study and fellowship. Also, with Kenneth, "We began having devotions in the morning. We don't pray out loud together real well, even now after twelve years, but we began to study the Bible together."

As they read the Bible, she found God speaking to her personally through the Word. "I would read these things and I would get so excited because I thought, 'That's me!' That's where the growth came, you know, beginning to read the Word, and it put its finger on me and said, 'This is you.'"

Their first crisis came after six months of marriage, when Kenneth broke his neck and Sally had to take care of him. A few months later, she had a miscarriage, which "felt like a loss of part of me. And yet I didn't grieve over it. I really had a peace; the Lord was really strong; it was a growing time." Harder than losing the baby was the cold shoulder she got from her sister and other friends. "They avoided me because they thought they would hurt me by being pregnant themselves, which was not the case. It hurt me more that they wanted to avoid me than that they were going to have a baby." When their first baby did come some time later, Sally decided that she would not have been ready for the earlier one. "I just probably couldn't have handled it at that time. I have a tendency not always to walk by faith, and then later to see the Lord's purpose in it and be able to accept it."

Sally went on to describe other, more recent struggles and victories. Some close friends had let her down, and she had to come to terms with their fallibility and her own tendency to withdraw into herself to avoid getting hurt. She had to contend with feelings of bitterness, and trying hard to "forgive and forget." Her church could not hold its young people, and she felt discouraged because the efforts she and Kenneth had put into youth and young adult groups seemed to go for naught. "Kenneth keeps telling me, 'That's our role; maybe that is what God intends for us—to be there for these young people, to lead them to the faith, to bring them to a point where they can walk.'"

She feels the tension between being available to respond to needs outside the home and then feeling guilty for neglecting her family. She continues to struggle with the inner need to meet other people's expectations and her own lack of self-esteem. She doesn't feel her church offers the kind of spiritual guidance that she would like, and she is tempted to leave, but the steadfast loyalty of her husband holds her fast—at least for the present. "I finally gave it over to the Lord that when we're supposed to leave, he will move Kenneth's heart, and until then here I am. So I feel at peace with it."

Sally serves the Lord by teaching an adult Sunday school class. She also makes country crafts for sale, and sees her faith influencing this through her honest dealings with her customers and her refusal to sell on Sundays. Her faith has moved her to go to the school board to oppose a change to a full-day kindergarten which she did not feel was good for her daughter. She and Kenneth also support a mission camp for inner-city children.

From a teenage girl who wanted to die because she felt lonely, no good, and unloved, Sally Steele has grown by the grace of God and the love of her husband into a mature, dedicated, and faith-filled woman. She still battles against low self-esteem and feelings of isolation, but the warmth and sincerity she radiates, the witness she bears in her church and community, and her faithful seeking of the Lord in regular prayer and Bible study, are ample evidence of the redeeming power of Jesus Christ in a human life.

Questions for Thought and Discussion

1. What factors contributed to Sally's "new birth"? At what points was the Spirit of God moving in her life?

2. What part has the church played in Sally's faith journey? What might be done, either by her and Kenneth or by the pastor and other members, to make her congregation more effective in nurturing the faith of its young people?

3. What are the faith issues that Sally is currently facing? What advice would you give to help her move beyond her present situation?

4. In what ways has your faith been evoked by significant relationships? What persons have been most influential in your faith journey?

5. In what ways do you affect the faith life of those around you? How can you share your faith story in ways that will enable the persons you love to "become Christian"?

6. What can you, your family, and your church learn from Sally's story that will enhance your ability to foster growth in faith and discipleship?

3. MURIEL ONISHI: GOD HAD A PURPOSE FOR MY LIFE

After returning to Hawaii from being trapped in Japan during
World War II, Muriel Onishi went to church for the first time in eight
years. Grateful for having survived the American bombing attacks on
Tokyo, she exclaimed, "God must have had a purpose for my life!"
She recounts the experiences that led up to that moment of thanksgiving, and the gradual maturing of her faith that has taken place in
the forty years since.

"My Mother Did Her Best"

Muriel's parents were Japanese immigrants to Hawaii who started a
Japanese language school in a rural town on Oahu. Her mother had
graduated from the Hiroshima Jogakuin mission school, and so saw
to it that Muriel went to Sunday school. Her father fell ill and
returned to Japan for treatment, dying there when Muriel was only
nine. "So my mother stepped into his shoes and took over the
language school. She had two children to look after and the school to
carry on, and she did her best. I don't think she could have withstood
all that pressure without her Christian background. If she hadn't had
the Christian faith, she wouldn't have made it." This memory of her
mother's courage and steadfastness in earning a living and raising her
family in the face of difficult odds was to sustain Muriel later on when
she was undergoing trials herself.

Muriel's mother taught her Christian songs and encouraged her to
go to confirmation class and join the church. She remembers being
baptized at age seventeen, and the "Bible study and good times at
youth fellowship groups." Her youthful experience in the church was
a happy one, but her faith had not yet become real and vital to her.

"I Knew Somebody Was Watching Over Me"

Shortly after graduating from high school, Muriel fell ill, and like
her father, was sent to Japan for medical treatment. She lived with her
uncle, and stayed on to study in a women's art college. While there,
the war broke out, and because of her excellent English she was

conscripted to work as an interpreter in the Japanese military headquarters in Tokyo, monitoring American radio broadcasts. She "hated
what the Japanese had done at Pearl Harbor," and was anxious for the
safety of her mother and brother. It was not until months later that she
learned from a Red Cross listing that her mother, as a Japanese
language school principal, had been interned in a Texas internment
camp, and her brother had joined the U.S. Army.

For Muriel, "it was day-to-day survival. As the war went on I just
didn't expect to live because it was getting closer and closer to Japan,
and here I was right in the middle of the supreme command headquarters." There were many close calls in bombing raids. She went to
Hiroshima to visit relatives and her father's grave—just three months
before the atom bomb was dropped there. On the return trip the train
ahead of hers was bombed in a station, and she had to walk two-and-
a-half hours to the next station carrying her bags. Then, "when I
came back to Tokyo, that night there was a heavy raid and a big fire.
Incendiary bombs fell near my home and I ran."

Speaking of Hiroshima, she says: "I recall vividly the day Hiroshima was bombed. No one knew what this bomb was, but they
knew it was a new destructive force. No sooner had the bomb fallen
than people from all over rushed in to Hiroshima to search for the
bodies of families and relatives. In due time they became severely sick
from the exposure to radiation. An uncle of mine was one of them. He
searched through the ashes for his son who had died in the blast. The
radiation gradually disintegrated his internal organs and he died a few
years later. How frightening to think that I could have been a victim of
Hiroshima myself. If I had waited a couple more months I could have
been in that atomic bomb!"

Muriel still has some guilt feelings about her service to the Japanese
high command. "What I was doing in the headquarters was helping
the strategy of the Japanese warlords. But it was a matter of survival. I
felt terrible about doing it, yet we were under duress. There were
advantages, though, as the headquarters was the safest place to be,
and they had enough to eat. This must have been God's way of watching over me during those stressful war years." She found herself
asking, "Why me, God? Why are you sparing my life from all this
terrible destruction? I asked this same question over and over again,
as I thanked God for keeping me alive from one raid to another."

Muriel's uncle was hostile to Christianity, so she could never go to church during those eight years in Japan. "He was really a great uncle to me, but as far as the Christian religion was concerned he just despised it. Knowing that, I never mentioned going to church. I had letters from home talking about what happened in the church, and that was about the only contact I had with Christian friends. But I knew that somebody was watching over me. And when the war ended, I realized suddenly that my faith, deep within myself, was what sustained me." Muriel was forced to be a Christian incommunicado, and her faith was kept in hibernation during those eight years. But the experience of danger, fear, and deprivation served to release a huge sense of gratitude for the protective presence of God with her during all that time.

"A New Life Began for Me"

Muriel had lost her American citizenship staying in Japan during the war, so had to return to Hawaii to reapply for it. The day she arrived, "The most miraculous thing really is that my friend came to visit me and took me to church that night. It was sort of a youth rally, and I remember the social hall was filled with all the young people. They welcomed me back, and it was such a wonderful feeling—as if I were born again at that moment. I had a strong sense that a new life was going to begin for me. On Thanksgiving, 1947, as I sat in church, I never felt so thankful that I was alive, that I had survived the whole ordeal. At that point I realized how grateful I was, and that there must have been a purpose for my life. The more I thought about it, I owed everything to God. I suddenly realized, how terrible of me that I never went to church in Japan."

Her return to familiar surroundings, seeing old friends, and realizing how fortunate she was to be alive, evoked a range of feelings in Muriel—guilt for her part in the Japanese war effort, regret for having neglected her Christian roots, thanksgiving for the gift of life, joy at reunion with family and church friends, and hope for the new possibilities that now lay before her.

"Nurtured to Become Strong Lay People"

The church came to mean so much to Muriel that when a young Nisei ex-G.I. proposed, her reply was, "If I agree to marry you, will

you promise to attend church with me every Sunday?" She had met
Harold in Japan after the war, where he was serving in the American
occupation forces. He was also from Hawaii, and had witnessed the
December 7 attack from the hills overlooking Pearl Harbor. He had
been introduced to Christianity by a Chinese couple with whom he
had had business ties before the war, but was still a staunch Buddhist
when he met Muriel. After being discharged, he returned to Hawaii,
looked her up, agreed to her condition, and they were soon married.

So, Muriel and Harold entered into the life of the church together.
"Everything was beginning to fall into place; I was getting active in
the church again." The pastor who married them asked Muriel to
teach Sunday school, and she started attending the women's society.
She became a local officer, then district secretary for spiritual life,
which led to her going to the regional school of mission.

There, "because they knew I spoke Japanese, they asked me to say
grace in Japanese during a meal. So I said okay; midway I paused,
and everybody said amen. I hadn't even finished my prayer, but I
just couldn't continue. It was a funny joke later on. I thank the Lord
for the many opportunities, which really helped me to grow." This
recognition as a leader, travel away from home, and blending of her
faith with her cultural identity made a profound impact on Muriel
and led her into a deeper, more articulate faith.

Muriel went on to hold "just about every office I can think of in our
local church." Although she and Harold attended the English congregation, she made a special effort to support the Japanese congregation in the same building, especially the new immigrants. With·
her congregation she is also engaged in the ministry to the street
people in Honolulu, serving soup every week for many years.

In recent years she has been concerned about peace issues. "I feel
very strongly about the present world situation. I don't want to see
another Hiroshima, because I've seen it. So by studying, by getting
involved in mission, I feel that I can help spread the word and try to
avoid another war. It seems fruitless to contend with our leaders, but
maybe by being friendly with our so-called enemies, or even within
our homes and communities, we can be ambassadors for peace."

A significant influence in her spiritual life was one pastor who
stayed ten years. "He was really caring. His sermons seemed like he
was talking to each one of us. It meant a lot to me. He really built up
this church; he kept us together. He nurtured us to become strong

laypeople. I remember when I had to do my first program as district spiritual life secretary, I went to his home and he actually sat down and we put our worship service together. In the groups that he led, he taught us to pray and develop our devotional lives. Because he built my foundation as a Christian layperson, I'm a stronger person in the faith."

Muriel and Harold are now in their sixties and seventies respectively, retired, but still active in their church. When speaking of the present point in her faith journey, she says: "As long as you have faith in Christ, nothing is impossible. As we grow, the church becomes more important to us. I feel that God has had a purpose for my life. So I'm willing to give up anything to do my share for God and the church."

As Muriel Onishi looks back over her journey, she is conscious of the guiding hand of God in it all. Through the influence of a courageous mother, disruptive events, and sensitive, caring pastors, and by virtue of her own growing awareness and willingness to serve, she has experienced a gradual maturing faith that gives every indication of keeping right on.

Questions for Thought and Discussion

1. What parallels and contrasts do you find between Muriel's faith journey and yours? Could you tell others about your journey as she has done?

2. How would you characterize the way(s) in which the Spirit of God was working in her life?

3. What further questions would you want to ask Muriel if you had a chance?

4. How would you have reacted if you had been in Muriel's shoes in Japan during the war?

5. What can your church learn from Muriel's story about ways and means of fostering faith and discipleship?

6. Do you believe that God has a purpose for your life, as Muriel does? If so, what is it, and how does this belief affect the way you live your life?

4. CARL SINN: I'VE GOT TO FIND AN ANSWER

When Carl Sinn was 64, out of the blue someone came along and offered to buy his lumberyard. "I wasn't ready to sell," he said, "but I thought, well, it's the only opportunity I might have to sell it, and it would give me a chance to do some of the things I really wanted to do. So I sold the yard, and before I knew it I was retired, and had lots of time on my hands. Then I began to think about what I wanted to do with my life." This sudden change of circumstance precipitated Carl into a search for religious meaning which has immensely enriched his life, led him deeper into the church, and has continued for almost ten years since that time.

Growing up in a Christian Family

Carl's parents were good moral people, and they sent him to Sunday school and church regularly. They themselves did not attend very much, however, except on special occasions, because they did not feel comfortable there. His father was a German immigrant and spoke in an interesting German-English brogue, while his mother was born in the United States of sturdy German immigrant stock. However, they taught Carl to be upright and hard-working. "From my mother I learned to be kind and thoughtful, and my dad taught me honesty and many good business tactics. When I was young I guess my main objective in life was to please other people. People would tell me the things they liked about me, which I thought was pretty nice. So I thought, well, the best thing to do is just try to make people like me more."

As a boy Carl attended church "50 to 75 percent of the time," was "taught that I should be good and honest," and learned the stories of the Bible. "I believed them 100 percent; I took them for granted and never questioned them." In his teen years, he was active in church, attended Epworth League, taught some classes, and went to youth camp. At nineteen, "I met a lady there who became my wife about a year later." He was active in the county Sunday School Association for awhile, but became discouraged and dropped out because he felt he had nothing to offer the organization. He remained involved in his local church for some time after that, but later "I just really lost interest because I figured I wasn't accomplishing anything."

Becoming a Workaholic

Carl was very ambitious as a young man. He worked in a bank for awhile, then bought the lumberyard, and organized an insurance agency. "I went to church probably 50 percent of the time, but I just wasn't enthusiastic. I tried to read a lot, but I could never find anything that really grasped me. Religion more or less fell by the wayside."

His business interests were occupying more and more of Carl's time. "I worked hard—long hours—and enjoyed my work. I became more or less a workaholic, I guess." When he worked on Sunday mornings, "I felt guilty, so I would take a back road home so I wouldn't have to go past the church."

A Change in His Thinking

As Carl approached sixty, "I noticed a change coming over my thinking. I got out of the idea that money was everything. I had been seeking security along secular rather than religious lines. But then, I began to find enjoyment in doing more for people than just taking their money. It became a real pleasure if I could do something they didn't expect in regular customer service, like unusual credit terms or special deliveries, just anything to try to help them out. As I went along, this change began to grasp me deeper and deeper."

It was then that the offer came to buy his lumberyard, which changed Carl's whole life direction. With his free time he began to read about and study the Christian faith. "The urge became stronger and stronger in me to learn more about Methodism and about the Bible. I never had been one to be able to get much out of reading the Bible. But now I discovered that to understand it I would have to do a lot of reading. So through the Sunday school books and other books that I found, I began to learn what all these passages meant, and the Bible became more and more important to me."

Carl became a voracious reader. "It seemed like from that time on God was just saying, 'Here, read this book, read that book,' and they just began to fall upon me. When I got through with one book, the first thing I knew, somebody suggested another one, just as if God had put that book into my hand and said, 'Here, read this.'"

He also began going to annual conference, and got involved in conference committees and other organizations beyond his local church. From this experience he learned much about the operation of the church, but also his eyes were opened to issues and interpretations which were new to him.

He began to question at a deeper level, and to seek answers. He returned to a quest that had begun years ago, but which he had put aside as he got involved in business. Carl describes it this way: "Like every young child, I accepted everything that people told me about the Bible. I believed that that was the way it was; I just took it for granted. Then, in my twenties, I began to question some of those things—the resurrection and all those miracles. Just how could that be? But then for several years I got really busy, and I more or less laid those thoughts aside." But when I got to be sixty, those thoughts started to come back to me. And I thought, 'Well, now, I've got to find an answer to these things—because I'm just not accepting them as they are. So that's one reason I began to read extensively, to find out just what those things were all about."

Three Levels of Faith

Before long, Carl did begin to discover some of the answers he was seeking. "I feel like I've grown," he says, "from the period of accepting on blind faith, through this period of testing when I questioned things, and now to some new levels in my faith. I have come at last to get some of the answers to what I should really believe. Just the last two or three years I've begun to grow as a Christian, and things have begun to gel. As I grow I find that I was lacking in so many things. I now know that being a Christian means believing in the teachings of Jesus as the best way to get closer to God, and becoming more like Jesus taught us to be."

For Carl there are three levels of being a Christian. First there is the "willingness to give to others and help them out, almost at any cost to yourself. All those years when I was so busy, I thought I was kind and generous, that I gave people things and did my part. But I realize now that I was really satisfying my own ego rather than doing it out of the generosity of my heart. Now I'm trying to put first things first by helping other people, rather than myself."

The second level is "doing work in the church. I had such a strong ambition to be able to get up and talk, to deliver a sermon, or to be a leader. I went to lay speakers' school and became a lay speaker. Then I began to realize that I was doing these things for myself rather than for the church or the people in it or for God. But now when I do those things I feel like I'm doing it for somebody else or the church, rather than for myself."

The third level for Carl is increased clarity and certainty in his beliefs and religious practices. For a long time he questioned things such as the resurrection and the virgin birth. He also wondered about why good people in other religions could not be saved just because they were not Christian. But he just put his doubts on hold. Recently he has been actively pursuing answers to these concerns. Now he has come to the conclusion that "by going directly to God with my prayers, and using the teaching of Jesus as an example," he is being faithful, and that "the Christian religion is the best way to get close to God." At the same time he respects persons of other faiths. He also thinks and reads a lot about the Christian faith. And, he exclaims, "It just fills my heart with joy so much of the time that I feel like my chest is going to explode!" Carl is experiencing the presence of God in his life, and it is affecting his behavior, his motivations, his thinking, and his inner sense of purpose and peace.

It is also affecting his attitudes and actions on community and social issues. He says that his growing faith has enabled him to become more open-minded and see the other side to issues such as abortion, war and peace, and apartheid in South Africa, in ways that were formerly not possible for him. Also, he has become "active in the cancer crusade and Lions Club, and some conference groups, and I write letters to Congressional representatives and senators once in awhile."

Carl's current goal is to begin to do some writing. As he explains it, "I find that I like to write about different experiences, to take just common ordinary things that you see each day and write a page or two or whatever it takes to get the point across. I feel that I have lots of good ideas people might like to read." He has taken a creative writing course in a local community college, and plans to devote more time to putting down his thoughts in this way. He teaches an adult Sunday school class, and this keeps him digging in the scriptures and other books on a regular basis. But this only whets his appetite for more communication about the faith, and he sees writing as a possible new outlet for this.

Carl Sinn sums up his religious quest this way: "When a person is young, he can't think too much along these lines. He becomes involved with marriage and children and business and all of that, and he doesn't have too much time. But when I was sixty years old, I knew there was something in my life that wasn't right, and I began to think after that. If you're fortunate enough to live into your sixties and seventies, you can look back and begin to put the pieces together and grow as a Christian."

Questions for Thought and Discussion

1. In what ways does your faith journey involve a search for God or for answers? What are some of the questions that puzzle you? With what group in your church could you share these?

2. Does your church encourage persons to seek and question, or is there an explicit or implicit assumption that "good Christians should not doubt"?

3. Is it surprising to you that someone as old as Carl is still seeking and growing? What does his story suggest about the religious experience of older adults?

4. At what points in Carl's journey do you see God as being especially active? Doing what?

5. Are there ways that Carl could have avoided the long lean years in the middle of his life when he became preoccupied with work and material values?

6. How can the church help people like Carl continue growing in faith and discipleship during those middle years? Would a faith-sharing group be a possibility?

B. Communal Pathways

1. KATHRINE LAYCOCK: AFFIRMED THROUGH CONFIRMATION

"Our confirmation class met for two years on Saturday mornings. My pastor was at that time God to me. I was very fond of him. He expected a lot of us and we in turn learned a lot from him." So does Kathrine Laycock, now forty-five, describe the experience at ages twelve and thirteen that was the most formative of her religious life. She goes on to explain: "The catechism process we went through was very rigorous. We were expected to memorize the Heidelberg Catechism from beginning to end. We also had long units on church history and the Bible, and long homework assignments. The tradition in the church was that there was a public examination on Palm Sunday, and then on Easter we were given first Communion with our families in front of the congregation. That was a very significant experience for me. I felt a strong commissioning, kind of becoming a disciple, and a part of that was taking Communion. I had this feeling that I was joining the band, that I was now one of the faithful."

At the age of thirteen Kathrine was experiencing a very personal awareness of belonging to the people of God. "I remember feeling it strongly at the time. It had been a long, hard time of preparation. I had been brought up close to the church. I loved the pastor. I had felt very affirmed through the process. He made it seem like a very personal journey. I felt that this was my commissioning service."

From Birth to Birth: Involved in the Church

From this point on, Kathrine had a different relationship to the church. Prior to confirmation she was a Sunday school student; afterwards she became an active church member, taught in the church school, and began singing in the choir.

Kathrine had been brought up in the church. As she puts it, "The church was the center of our family life, and I was expected to be in worship on Sunday morning. It was good, because the family was there."

In high school Kathrine was a leader in the youth fellowship, and in college the campus Christian fellowship became "a kind of stabilizing influence in my life. Being away from home for the first time, the church became my home. I always felt that no matter where I was, the church would be a place where I was accepted and comfortable." In this group, "There was a need for me and tasks to do, and that made it a comfortable transition and gave purpose to those college years above and beyond the classroom work."

After college Kathrine took a teaching job, and that summer was married to Frank Laycock, a high school teacher whom she had met while doing her practice teaching. Speaking of what attracted them to each other, Kathrine says: "We had some common visions and purposes for life, and recognized quickly that we wanted to continue that together. We both had put the church at the center of our lives and found that to be unique in people our age."

After their marriage, Kathrine and Frank served as church youth leaders for three years in her home church, then moved when she became pregnant and transferred their membership to a Methodist church near their new home—"close enough so we could really be involved, and so it would be convenient for our family to walk to church."

Confirmation Again: A Teacher Affirmed

Within months after their first child was born, their pastor invited Kathrine to teach Sunday school, something she has been doing ever since. Far from resenting this request so soon after joining a new church, Kathrine reflects, "It was a very welcoming kind of experience into that congregation." However, because she "felt shaky" about theology, she told the pastor, "Well, if that's what's needed, okay, but I'm going to start with two-year-olds."

From that point on she moved up through the age groups of the church school, keeping pace with her growing children. "That was really neat," she says. "Every three years or so I'd think, now I'm ready to learn the next level, and I'd move on. I took every level in the church school. I loved teaching in the church!"

The real satisfaction for Kathrine, though, came "about six years ago when I was approached to teach confirmation." She felt genuinely honored to be asked to play the same significant role in the lives of young people as her pastor of twenty-five years ago had played in hers. "It was a real affirmation to have a pastor appreciate what I had gone through to get to that point, to see that I had trained myself to be able to talk about my faith in a way that made me able to communicate with junior highs in a confirmation class. I liked that very much, and I have been comfortable doing that ever since."

Leadership in the Church: Linked in Ministry

As the years moved on, Kathrine became active in other aspects of church life—president of United Methodist Women, chairperson of education and the Council on Ministries, and lay leader. George was also an active church leader, "so we were still linked together in ministry and supported one another. The church was the place where we wanted to be, and so if we had babysitting money it was for Board meeting. We found this to be a really significant way to live our lives."

Frank and Kathrine have been members of this same congregation for the past eighteen years, and have seen much turnover of membership in that time. "That's part of the ministry of our church," she explains. As a suburban church, we "see ourselves as a church for people in transition. The turnover was very upsetting until we claimed it as ministry. We decided to try to strategize for people in transition for the two or three years they are here. That was a turning-around time for us."

Relationships with Pastors; Affirmation and Burnout

Several changes of pastors have taken place during these years. The pastor of her confirmation years has remained the model against which she measures other clergy. As she describes it, "That pastor provided an affirmation and a constant love that I needed and did not receive at home. I trusted him implicitly, and he trusted me. So when I think of God as being a constant presence in my life, I think about qualities that were in that man, who helped me to see what I understand God to be in my life now."

The pastor who asked Kathrine to teach confirmation was another with whom she formed a significant relationship. He understood her faith struggles, gave her books that stretched her and fed her appetite for new theological insights, and counseled her in dealing with some pressing family problems.

But more recently, another change of pastors has sent her into a time of testing: "I have some feelings that are mixed up and negative, and have felt a lot of concern for our congregation. During this time of turmoil, we have hung in there and worked harder than ever in order to maintain the ministry that had been going on in that church. But when we didn't receive the kind of support and sense of mutual ministry we were used to, we began to feel a little burned out. So I decided to create some space for myself. I was very open with the pastor, and told him I was going to pull back in order to have some time to think about what was going on."

So Kathrine resigned from her church positions and took some months by herself to "unscramble all these things that have happened." Then, later, she began to move out of her "desert time," and into a period of renewed energy and commitment. "I am ready to rededicate myself to my belief in God, my sense of being part of the word-deed community, and what discipleship means in my life," is the way she put it.

A Growing Faith: Both Individual and Corporate

Although Kathrine's faith journey is centered in the church, she also, from early childhood, has had "a feeling of a personal relationship with God. When things didn't go smoothly at home, and when I went through shaky times, there was always something I could turn to that would offer me assurance that I was an okay person. I called that God. I would draw away for quiet times, and then I could turn back to whatever I was doing, and go on and live my life.

"Later, when I went through confirmation I began feeling a relationship with Christ. If I really wanted to understand this power that I felt in my life, I needed to take a good look at Jesus, the Christ. Then, with my first Communion, discipleship and servanthood became clear to me. I felt a close relationship with God, and there were many times when I would go into the church sanctuary by myself and feel that solitary experience which was a running strand through my life."

Kathrine's awareness of being in relationship with God and a deep sense of belonging to the church continued through high school. "At that time," she reports, "I had to break away from my family to go to college, and that meant leaving my church. I can remember struggling with that. I pulled away by myself into the church sanctuary, and had this strong feeling that there would always be a congregation for me to relate to. I was aware of this promise through my relationship with God, and it has always been true for me." In describing her personal relationship with God, Kathrine still casts it in the context of belonging to a community of faith.

Confronted by Faith: Called to Be a Presence

A big test for Kathrine's faith came in relation to her younger brother and sisters. When they became caught up in the drug culture and the sexual revolution, it was to Kathrine that they often came for help. In her they found someone who would accept them and provide genuine caring and support.

This encounter with a different culture and lifestyle was a real shock to Kathrine, however. "The person they dumped on continually was me, and I had to deal with some real 'culture shock.' I was the one closest to them—the one who had taken care of them when I was younger—and when I observed them going through these lifestyle changes, there were times when I just didn't know how to deal with it. They were violating my moral standards, yet I knew I had to keep loving them. There was something inside me that said, 'If you don't want to lose those people, you've got to keep accepting them. Remember how God accepted you. You're on the line.' So I kept on being a presence, and I did not reject them through these experiences.

"I can remember one time my sister called when she was being threatened by a fellow with a hand gun. She had a baby at the time, and was involved in the drug scene. She was hysterical, and asked me to come get her because she was frightened for the baby. I turned to Frank and said, 'It's Kim, and she's in a lot of trouble. What should we do?' He just looked at me and said, 'What would Jesus do?' I said, 'Right.' So I told Kim, 'Just stay in the house and we'll be there to get you.'"

Through experiences like this Kathrine was "confronted by my faith," for she felt called and stretched to be an accepting, supportive presence for her brother and sisters in situations she had never faced before. And when she shared these concerns with her pastor, "He wasn't afraid of dealing with me about them, and he affirmed the way I handled it. So then I began to get some help from within the faith."

After a much needed period of prayer and reflection, Kathrine is ready for the next challenge that God has to offer her. What will it be? Whatever it is, Kathrine is excited about the prospects.

Questions for Thought and Discussion

1. What factors have been most influential in Kathrine's faith journey?

2. How can the church best nurture the faith of people such as Kathrine? What setting could be provided in which they could share their questions and struggles with one another?

3. Does your church's confirmation program make the kind of impact on your young people that Kathrine's did on her? What could be done to help this happen more consistently?

4. At what points do you find yourself resonating most with the way Kathrine expresses her faith? Where would you have a different interpretation of events or religion than she does?

5. How does Kathrine's story challenge you to share your story with others?

6. How would you have handled the situation that Kathrine faced with her younger brother and sisters? What faith resources would you have drawn on to help you in this?

2. BRUCE COPELAND: EVANGELIZING THE INSTITUTION

Representative of a small but significant group of Christians whose faith is developed and expressed primarily through the challenge of service and social action is Bruce Copeland, financial consultant and real estate agent in a large metropolitan area. Bruce refers to his midlife transformation in faith as the shift from a "Boy Scout ethic" to the "ethic of justice."

"Morbus Sabbaticus"

The son of a Presbyterian minister in the East, Bruce had a typical church upbringing—church attendance, blessing before meals, study of the catechism, memorization of Bible verses, and "a temperance union for kids on Sunday afternoon where we would take the pledge after somebody made a speech about the horrors of alcohol." He describes his childhood as "pretty traditional." "We were expected to go to Sunday school and church. I don't remember rebelling, though occasionally we got 'morbus sabbaticus,' a special illness that would occur on Sunday morning when we didn't want to go. But mostly, we just kind of went along with it."

In college Bruce kept up the church-going habit. "I didn't get involved in any other activities; it was just going out of a sense of duty—this is what you're supposed to do on Sundays." Leaving college to enter the Navy during World War II, Bruce "probably shifted into neutral for two or three years," as far as faith and church were concerned.

But while stationed on the West Coast, he attended a young adult group in a Congregational church. "So it was the young people's group there that got me back into the church. They had a camp and went on retreats, which was kind of neat. And they had some discussion of issues, but not very compelling. It was probably more of a social experience."

There he met Carol, his future wife. "We met around Christmas time, got engaged at Easter, and were married in August in that church. Then we went back to the Midwest for me to finish my last year of college." Back in college, Bruce recalls the impact of a Bible teacher. "I had one professor of Bible I liked; he was pretty good in terms of instruction. But there was no strong religious thing going on. He just seemed interested in us as individuals. I don't remember what he taught us—no content or concepts. It was mainly his own personal warmth and interest." Perhaps Bruce was not yet ready for serious examination of the content of his faith. But the incarnated caring of a Christian teacher touched him with a reminder of the essence of the Christian faith—love.

"The Boy Scout Ethic"

After graduation Bruce and Carol moved to the East Coast, got a job in an insurance company, and went to a Congregational church. "Within about two Sundays I ended up chairing the every member canvass. I was twenty-two years old, and they must have been in dire straits because it was about a five or six hundred-member congregation. I struck up a conversation with the pastor, and he recruited me on the spot. I'd never done anything like that, so I read some materials and talked to some people to prepare myself." Perhaps this incident says something about Bruce's leadership ability and readiness to get involved, as well as about the sensitivity of this pastor to cultivate his gifts, when still so new to the congregation.

Bruce describes their experience in this church as follows: "We went to church every Sunday. That was a warm experience. The pastor preached a pretty good sermon. They had a good choir. It was a pretty church in an old New England setting. We were just getting started. We had our first child there. We were picking up on what we had done in our younger days, but now we were adults. There was nothing special about it. It was socializing, meeting people. The church had a softball team, and I played second base and pitcher. This was a throwback to the church of my youth, where we had a very active softball league. So it was that kind of social experience.

"We were there about two-and-a-half years. We remained active in that church. I got involved in the financial program, and Carol was in one of the women's groups. There was no connection yet with what I was doing in my vocation. Still a pretty traditional approach to Christianity—what I call the Boy Scout ethic: be trustworthy, kind, and tell the truth, with a bit of Golden Rule added in." Viewed from the perspective of his mature faith nearly forty years later, Bruce tends to minimize this, his first adult church experience. But it was formative for him, in the sense of establishing the pattern of their adult lives—regular, active participation—which kept him available to the continued influence of the gospel in his life.

The Copelands' next move took them back to California—a new opportunity for Bruce in his insurance company. "The week we got there a pastor called on us who was just starting a brand new church. So we were among the first ten charter members of that group, mainly young ex-G.I.s and their families. I got involved in fund--

raising to put up the first building. It was a very vigorous time for the next few years, starting that church. We built three or four buildings. We had mortgages on mortgages. I was the one going out to make all kinds of financial deals; it was very exciting."

In this church Bruce also began to learn that there was more to the Christian faith than the Boy Scout ethic. "The pastor provided my first experience with raising social issues. He took a slightly more nontraditional approach to peace. Once a year we had a symposium with a speaker on some significant issue. My consciousness was beginning to be raised about the inadequacy of the Boy Scout ethic."

In helping to start this new congregation, Bruce had made a heavy investment of time and energy in the work of the church. He found satisfaction in being part of a successful and growing enterprise, and in beginning to discover the implications of the Christian faith for more of life than simply Sunday religious activities. The seed had been sown and was starting to grow.

A Focus on Stewardship

The first sign of Bruce beginning to relate his faith to his work life took place in connection with his insurance business. "I was selling life insurance, and doing estate planning and money management with people." His pastor told him that in marital counseling one of the chief problems he was running into was tension over money. He asked Bruce to develop a system for helping couples manage their money. The plan he worked out was so effective that it came to the attention of both his insurance company and the national stewardship office of his denomination, and was widely utilized. Bruce describes it this way:

"They were raising the question of how the national church could help the local church on the issue of stewardship—not simply how to get the pledges in, but helping people manage their money. At the same time, in my business I was finding that people were saying, 'I think I need that insurance, but I can't afford it. So if you can show me where I can get the premiums, then I'll buy the insurance. So all these things were intersecting, and I was beginning to develop some techniques for this. We had a series of four or five classes on managing your money as a Christian. I was trying to find ways for people to be better stewards of their money. In the course and with my clients I also talked about wills: 'Have you considered leaving anything to a church or charity?' There were several million dollars in potential bequests that I was instrumental in arranging over the years. Here was another linkage that I was making between my faith and my work life.

"I had grown up with a family that tithed. Carol and I weren't able to initially, but we moved in steps to a tithe by the time we were twenty-five or twenty-six, and we've over-tithed almost ever since. I think of stewardship as a responsible use of your funds, not just how much you give to the church. I had a pattern I used in speeches to our company conventions—you give enough first, you save enough next, and you live off the balance. If your bank account is low you just eat hot dogs for awhile. I was pretty successful in getting people to think in those terms. So here again I was trying to make a connection. My faith was beginning to move into my business operation."

From a local church every member canvass, to money management training for church couples, to a denominational financial planning and stewardship program, to a giving emphasis in his insurance counseling, to talks on stewardship to his company convention—step-by-step Bruce Copeland was making a more direct and intentional expression of his faith.

Outreach to the Community

Once transferred to a larger California city where Bruce became manager of a new branch office, he moved beyond church and stewardship manifestations of his faith to active involvement in the community. "My view of doing good, let's say, was to get involved with one or two charitable organizations and try to help them."

In his previous community he had gotten a group of seventy doctors together to form a 200-bed private hospital, and was chairperson of the board. Now, in his new location, "I got together the Congregational and Episcopal churches, who had never previously related to one another, at the level of putting up a retirement home with nursing facilities. These homes were being built in other communities on cheap land in the country. We had a vision of old folks wanting to be in town where they could walk to church and the drugstore, or get on a bus and go see their friends and families. So I did that, and part of it was my Christian conscience saying I should."

At this point in the story Bruce paused to reflect on what all this was adding up to: "You know, I'd been encouraged in my early years to consider being a pastor. But for some reason I didn't want to do that. I remember saying to my mother, 'I decided to be a good Christian layperson, and act out my Christian faith that way rather than being a fulltime pastor.' So there is still some of that, and it comes through once in awhile."

Involved in the Issues

Next Bruce and Carol moved their family back East where he became an executive in a large insurance company. They started going to a large Presbyterian church, but "it was a bust. The guy was going to retire in a couple of years, and nothing was going on." The stage was set for a radicalization of Bruce's faith through a series of events that turned his life around. It was 1965.

"We happened to go to a Vietnam forum in a little Baptist church. It was a Sunday night, and the American Legion and John Birch Society came out in uniform, carrying banners and flags. They screamed and hollered and broke up the meeting. There were 200 people there trying to hear something. We decided there must be something going on there, so we started going to that church.

"That was the beginning of a major shift in our perceptions of what our faith was about. These folks had a very active adult education program, and an early service in the contemporary mode. They had three or four black families and two Asian, and they were very involved in the issues.

"At the time of Martin Luther King's assassination, we had a big uproar when the Board of Deacons asked the church to mortgage itself for $100,000 and give it away to the urban crisis. So on a Sunday morning we met for five-and-a-half hours with several long-time members threatening to leave the church if we did this, hotly debating the issue. In the final vote we had 74 percent in favor of doing it. Most of us were elated. We lost six members over this—and gained fifty-four. It was amazing. The word got out, and we got national attention about this little Baptist church that was going to mortgage itself. We asked community groups to present proposals, and we would screen them and vote on them. It proved to me that the local church could take a position on some issues without going bankrupt."

Bruce was having his consciousness raised about the church's engagement in mission to his own city and neighborhood. And he was excited about it. He went on to describe other issues in which his church became involved: "We invited a gay pastor to preach, and he started his sermon by saying, 'I'm gay and I'm proud.' He told about his experience and how painful it was. I hadn't known anything about the issue of homosexuality before that. We went across to a coffee house between services and discussed it in a talk-back time. I said, 'It could be really tough if you were both black and homosexual.' And our black pianist said, 'Wouldn't it be really tough if you were black and a woman and homosexual in our society!' And after that she came out, walking across the street with her woman friend. That morning was quite an experience for me! And that congregation was ready to deal with the issue.

"We had black power people come out from their inner city ghetto and really bang away at the church. Through them we experienced the rage of the black community. We went into their ghetto, and I became involved in rehabilitating housing. We built one three-flat, then turned the building over to the public housing authority, because we were unsuccessful in getting community people to take over the organizational leadership. The project was a partial failure, but we learned a lot. We got on buses and went to Washington to protest marches, and this was also very exciting. All these ventures were a corporate ministry. It was the church as a body, or as individuals, out in the world trying to do good."

Bruce had moved another significant step forward in his understanding of the ministry of the laity in the world. He had become involved in a vital congregation that was engaged with the real issues of its day and place. He was being challenged to live his faith in the secular world, regardless of the extent of controversy and risk.

An Inside Change Agent

Next Bruce became involved with an ecumenical urban mission program in his city. This began when he heard the co-director "give a speech to a group of thirty of us business people: 'The new gospel message is to evangelize the institutions. That's where the power and injustice are. If we believe in justice, we've got to change the structures. Your job is to go into situations where you have influence, especially where you work, and try to bring about change. That's your Christian responsibility.' He challenged us to preach the gospel to our institutions. That was a mountaintop experience for me—one of only three or four in my whole life. It brought about a major shift in my life. From that moment on I started a whole new lay ministry emphasis. I said to myself, 'Gee, that's what I should be doing instead of spending my time with just the United Way or YMCA. I should be involved with challenging my company.'"

The changes Bruce helped bring about in that big company were remarkable. Viewing himself as an "inside change agent," he put together a group of four other people at different levels in the organization to strategize and work for change. Their goal was to bring women and blacks into the company and move them into positions of leadership. They were supported at first by the president. Funds were made available to bring the urban mission staff in as consultants. Women and minorities were sought, hired, trained, and promoted. One woman, still in her mid-twenties, became an officer and department head.

All this time Bruce was meeting with the urban mission staff and other Christian laity. "The goal was to work with us to do our work inside our institutions. We would meet once every couple of weeks for two or three hours to discuss strategy. We got ideas, did visioning and planning, and learned techniques for problem solving. Always the agenda was how to change the institution into something just.

"In my company, my management style was very participatory, with decision making shared from the lowest to the highest. We tried to get the company to deal with issues of ecology and a socially responsible investment strategy. We were working on values. We were fairly effective."

But the resistance to all this change was gradually building up in our company. "Our values impinged on other senior officers who were used to an autocratic management style. And they were unable to deal with women or minorities in positions of responsibility. They were used to filling all their management positions with white men. They complained to the president. One of the vice presidents had gone in and pounded on his desk and said, 'Bruce has got to go.' I was rocking the boat. When I suggested to the president that we senior managers get together with him to discuss issues of racism and sexism, he said to me, 'Bruce, this company is not a democracy; it's a monarchy, and I'm the king.' The following Tuesday I was dismissed by the president, who had been a friend for fifteen years. My woman associate was fired too. I had been with that company for ten years, and all of a sudden I was unemployed. I had tried to link my faith to my work, and I paid the price for it. I had the image of our little group of five people in a boat rowing upstream, and fifty rowing downstream. And the boat was going upstream! But after I left, the company reverted back to the old ways. That was the most disappointing part."

In the wake of his traumatic dismissal, Bruce was supported by his family, the urban ministry strategy team, and a lay ministry support group in his church. All met with him to debrief the experience and help him plan the next steps for his life.

A Continuing Lay Ministry in the World

Bruce was six months without a job, then moved to a Midwestern city to become president of a small insurance company. "I told them my values and goals, and they said, 'Fine, go ahead, as long as you get the job done.' So I began to make the same kinds of changes there— participatory decision making, affirmative action in employment, and promotion of women and minorities. Much happened along these lines in the three years I was there. Over half the technical and management staff became women and minorities."

But major illness intervened, and Bruce was forced temporarily to give up his ministry of "evangelizing the institution." He developed cancer, underwent chemotherapy, then got shingles and phlebitis. He was incapacitated for eighteen months. When he was well enough to work again, he decided to shift from insurance into real estate. His goal was "to see if I could apply the principles of justice to that business, another conservative financial institution."

In the years since he made this transition, Bruce has helped to form three not-for-profit housing development corporations to provide decent, affordable housing for limited income and handicapped persons. He also has helped develop group homes for the mentally retarded and shared apartment arrangements for the mentally ill. He has been instrumental in establishing a self-help organization for ex-mental patients. He has also organized a lay ministry support group in his local church, and continues to do money management counseling with lay people desiring to make socially responsible investments. He views selling real estate as a ministry, and provides free financial planning advice to his clients in order to help them invest wisely, give generously, and purchase housing within their means.

Looking back over his sixty-year faith journey, Bruce Copeland points to four "mountaintop experiences" that have influenced him significantly—hearing the urban mission director talk about ministry in the workplace, encountering the gay pastor, being confronted with "You're the problem" by inner city blacks, and hearing a talk on women's liberation. Each experience had led him to new awareness of the pain and oppression of a marginalized group. Each had challenged him to invest himself more deeply and vigorously in the ministry of social change. Each had helped him see new connections between his Christian faith and his life in the world.

Speaking of his personal spiritual life, Bruce says: "Recently I have come to see more connection between biblical themes and my social activity. My spiritual growth has been gained through the support and strength of being with people of faith, and through being challenged in emotional situations." Clearly, the Holy Spirit has worked with Bruce in dramatic ways, and has led him to a remarkable depth of commitment. "I guess it goes back to my upbringing. I inherited it through my genes from my mother and father, and socialization in my home. I was trained to do right—at first by the Boy Scout ethic, now by the ethic of justice."

His word to the church is: "The church should do what it says, practice what it preaches, go in and change things, bring about justice." Certainly, his credentials back up this admonition.

Questions for Thought and Discussion

1. What points in Bruce Copeland's story challenged you most deeply? Why? In what ways could the telling of your story be a challenge to others?

2. Do you see Bruce's approach to lay ministry as a model for others to follow? Why or why not?

3. How would you have responded had you, like Bruce, been fired for working for justice in your company?

4. Where in the Bible do you find a basis for Bruce's understanding of the ministry of the church and its members?

5. How can your church best challenge, train, and support the laity for their ministry in the world? What does Bruce's experience suggest in this regard? Could a faith-sharing and ministry strategy group like Bruce experienced be developed in your church?

6. How do you respond to Bruce's word to the church: "Practice what you preach, go in and change things, bring about justice"?

3. BILL AND MARILYN HOGG:
THE TWO BECOME ONE—IN WITNESS

Bill and Marilyn were both Army officers when they met and fell in love. She was "praying for a Christian husband," and he "wanted to date and marry a Protestant girl, because it was important that we be of the same faith." Bill's faith up to that point had been a rather intellectual, though active, Presbyterianism, while Marilyn had "accepted God at the altar" of a one-room country Methodist church at the age of nine, and was quite a zealous evangelical Christian.

Marilyn's view of marriage, which has had a strong influence on their life and faith from that day to this, was a literal interpretation of "the two shall become one." Bill describes it this way: "The thing that determined that we were going to grow together was her understanding that the two shall become one flesh. We are not two separate entities any more; we're one. And so we grew together; as we went to church, we went together."

Marilyn responded, "Yes, but you have become the dominant one, which pleases me greatly. You've always been the leader. You are such a faithful servant of the Lord. If I were to fall, you would pick me up. Also, you are such a committed person—not only to me but to the Lord. I know you've grown more fundamental as we've lived together. You have a great understanding of the Bible, much greater than mine. When we were first married I was the one who was always bringing out the Bible. Now you may very well be the first to do so."

Bill and Marilyn Hogg were the only persons of the forty-four who insisted on being interviewed together. From the time they met and married, their faith journeys have been merged into one. Each has respected the other's faith commitment; each has been strengthened by the other's faith expression; and together their life in home, church, and community has been a witness to the power of Jesus Christ to heal and transform lives. For both, the primary influence in leading them to a deeper faith experience has been participation in small, intimate Christian groups, especially in Lay Witness Missions.

Bill Hogg: Basketball and Envelopes

Bill was taken to a nearby Baptist church as a small boy, but in seventh grade switched to the Presbyterian in order to play basketball in the church league. Required to attend church to stay eligible, he became impressed with the pastor who could speak Greek and "preached well-structured, intellectual sermons." In the eighth or ninth grade, "I found out that all the guys were going to the confirmation class, so I went too. We went through our usual four or five weeks on Sunday afternoon, and on Palm Sunday we joined the church. This didn't have any special significance, other than that now I was a member, and now I got envelopes! I continued to go to church regularly, and the church was a part of my life. And I remember marveling at the minister being able to get a sermon ready every week; that was really something; he had to say something interesting. But I can't say that I was a zealous Christian. At that point I didn't really recognize what it meant to commit oneself to Jesus Christ, for life. But I know it was the thing to do."

Bill went on to college and was very active in the church there. "It was purely a student church—all the members and officers except the pastors were students. I was ordained a deacon in the Presbyterian Church at the age of twenty. I went to church, ushered, and became involved in activities, but it never really had a whole lot of effect on the way I lived my life. I cannot remember at that time ever having heard a specific call, that there was something specific required for salvation. I knew about Jesus, and that he died for my sins, and I knew the Easter story and the Virgin Birth. I had no reason to doubt any of that. But it never became personalized or internal; it was just a belief. That's what the Bible said, and that's what you believed. And I kept the faith." Bill was a faithful Christian, both in belief and in practice, during those years.

"After college I went into the Army. And I went to church in the Army. I guess I was fairly unique. There was an Army chapel on the base, but I didn't care for that too much, so I went to a church in town. I don't really know why I kept going to church in the service. I certainly wasn't considered a religious kook. It's got to be the Lord's hand in it, because there's nothing I can think of, on my own, that would have led me to stay with the church." Bill continued with his faithful Christian habits on into early adulthood. It was at this point that he met Marilyn.

Marilyn Hogg: Family Influences and Major Illness

In contrast to Bill's, Marilyn's faith journey prior to their meeting had been tumultuous and eventful. Born and raised on a farm, she had a lonely and deprived childhood, which in retrospect was also rich in that "I was alone with the Lord a great deal." A primary influence was a maiden aunt who taught school in the city and came home on weekends. "She believed in the Lord with all her heart and soul, taught me to read and write before I went to school, and read the Bible to me." Her aunt also set an example of Christian living for little Marilyn to emulate, as, for instance, when she gave her fur coat to a poor woman in the city.

"This aunt died when I was six years old, and I felt alone, with no one in the world but God and me, because no one could understand my hurt. God was the only one who could understand, so I felt that God was a real comforter with the Holy Spirit. It was a real, living experience within me." Other important influences were her mother, who "went to church regularly and believed totally in the Lord," and her father, who "did not go to church but taught me some of the best things that I learned, because he was such a good man."

Another kind of family influence that deeply affected Marilyn was a deep-seated conflict between her father and grandfather. Her grandfather considered her father a foreigner and did not accept him, even though they lived on his farm. "My father loved my mother very much, and he tried not to have any confrontations. My grandfather would hold me on his lap and be loving to me, but then he would reject my father which was like a rejection of me."

Eventually Marilyn's father left the family to put a stop to the conflict. "My parents did not separate, but my father went to work somewhere else and we would visit him. Then, after my grandfather died, we got together as a family again. My father evidently left for my mother's sake, and he didn't attend my grandfather's funeral, just because of that terrible animosity. So you can understand, I was trying to figure out the meaning of life. I loved both in my way, and I had to have an answer to the enigma of how people could be so cruel to one another, and still be good people. I had to have an answer from God, for myself.

"This was a very difficult family situation; it was overwhelming to me as a child. So I went to the altar and poured it out, and I accepted Christ. I remembered going to a back room and crying. My mother was with me, and the minister, talking with me, wanting me to tell what I had done—accepted Jesus. This was a meaningful thing to me." Family conflict had precipitated a crisis in Marilyn's life, which led her at the age of nine to open her heart to Christ.

The third factor in Marilyn's early life that influenced her faith journey was a major illness after she graduated from college. "I got very sick with hepatitis, and was a bedpan patient in the hospital for three months. When I lay in that hospital, I was alone again—totally alone with God. And I just communed with him every day, and he healed me for some reason—so that I could bear witness to him."

Conversion Through a Lay Witness Mission

These early experiences of Marilyn sound very much like a scenario in the pathway which is "awakened through crisis and turmoil." And her story by itself could well be classified there, except for the fact that after her marriage to Bill their life together took a somewhat different turn. They became Presbyterians because that was his church ("There wasn't any question, if that's the husband's religion, then it's the wife's, too," was the way she put it.), and continued growing in the faith.

Bill describes their experience this way: "We grew because we continued in the church. We were always active in the church, and our activities continued to broaden. We got exposed to a lot of different kinds of preaching. But the Presbyterian Church is not really big on a personal commitment to Christ. Corporate worship is the main thing, and it is basically a non-emotional response to God.

"But we met a few people, both within and outside the Presbyterian church, some of whom were active in the Fellowship of Christian Athletes. They had a little different perspective; it was a more personal faith. Then we started going to a Christian couples' club, which was a nondenominational, very evangelical group, that would meet every month or two, have a good speaker, and give testimonies. I had never heard testimonies in my life; I didn't know what a testimony was. I'd never seen an altar call.

"We held a Lay Witness Mission in our church, and it was really my turning point—not when I accepted Christ; I had accepted Christ at some point earlier. But people were talking about, 'I've accepted Christ,' and I was thinking, 'Well, yeah, I've heard all that. I guess I've accepted Christ; I mean I haven't rejected him, and I know he died on the cross for me.' But it was starting to mean different things to me.

"The Lay Witness Mission is a fairly intense weekend. The final Sunday builds up to an altar call. I was general chairperson; I was responsible for this whole weekend. We had a very dynamic coordinator, and he gave an altar call that Sunday. I thought, 'Oh, Lord, he's not going to give an altar call in a Presbyterian church!' But you know, when he gave the call you couldn't keep me in my seat. I had to go forward. The weekend was getting to me; it was really an experience. I thought, 'I don't know what's going to happen, but I've got to go up there.' And after I was up there, I looked around and half the church was up there. Through that experience I realized that it's all right to be emotional, it's okay to feel this faith, and it's all right to go out and witness to it. And I got a new meaning in my faith.

"Three weeks later we were out on a Mission, and I got called on to give my testimony. It was a brand new experience for me. I'd only seen it once or twice, and now here I was doing it. That was fifteen years ago, and since then Marilyn and I have gone on dozens— maybe fifty—Lay Witness Missions. It has become a very important part of our lives."

Healing in a Charismatic Fellowship

About that time Bill and Marilyn also became involved in a charismatic fellowship meeting in an Episcopal church. Bill continues: "We became interested in the baptism of the Holy Spirit at that point, and we started attending a Wednesday night meeting. It was at this fellowship that Marilyn's back was healed. I mean literally. She was in bed, hardly able to move, and we went there, and it was healed."

Marilyn picks up the story at that point. "They even had to turn my head in bed. I was in terrible shape. I had had this injury; they said I was going to have to have a spinal fusion. So we were desperate. Bill got me to the altar; I can't remember how he got me there, but he was determined. And there was a laying on of hands by the minister and the elders and other people. And I turned from that altar and walked down. I was totally healed—from not being able to turn my head and back."

That was the first of two remarkable healing experiences that Marilyn has had. The second came "three years ago when I was diagnosed as having cancer of the uterus. The night before the operation I put my life in God's hands. If I were to live, God would make known to me what I was to do. If not, I was prepared to die. When I was in prayer that night, I told the Lord, 'I'm ready to die if you want me to come now, but if there's something else for me to do, please tell me what it is.' And as clear as I'm talking, I heard the words, 'Lay Witness Mission.'

"The next morning when I went into the operation, I was totally alone with God again. Well, they found no cancer when they went in there. So I believe with all my heart that God is alive, here with me, that there's no question that God is our companion. Since then Bill and I have dedicated our lives to going on Lay Witness Missions, because we have no doubt that God told us to do that. I believe that the Holy Spirit is within us. We have totally turned our lives over to the Lord, and the Lord has empowered us with the Spirit."

Bill confirms this testimony. "We have both received the baptism of the Holy Spirit. We did receive an anointing from the Holy Spirit, did speak in tongues, and still do occasionally. It's not a big thing, but it's part of who we are."

A Life of Witness

In the years since these significant formative events, the Hoggs' life together has been characterized by one central theme—witness. They have conducted many Lay Witness Missions. Now members of a United Methodist church, they have both become certified lay speakers, and have held a variety of church offices—currently evangelism co-chairpersons. Recently they have begun a ministry in a local nursing home, conducting weekly worship services and visiting the residents in their rooms with prayer and friendly conversation.

When Marilyn's brother's wife deserted her family some years ago, and her brother "couldn't handle it," the Hoggs took in their eight children—all at one time, and have raised them all. Their home became a witnessing environment to these children and their friends. Marilyn describes it thus: "We always went around the table with all these children, reading the books of the Bible—that was our ritual. And Dad would teach the Bible to them. And there was a neat game about who says the prayer tonight, so that they did enjoy learning their prayers that way, at the table. Every morning we had devotions, and every night we said prayers together before we went to sleep. And we often had prayer at noon, too."

Most of the Hoggs' children have also participated in Lay Witness Missions, and several have come to Christ through this influence. Says Bill: "With at least three of our children, the youth mission part of Lay Witness Mission has been instrumental in their coming to Christ. Our youngest daughter goes on Missions with us now, and she's one of our leaders in the youth group. This is a fine way of bringing youth to Christ, because it's youth who have met Christ sharing with other youth. All of our kids have been touched through the Missions, and three have really come to know Christ in a personal way through them."

Marilyn also describes her witness to friends and young people in her home. "Whenever anyone would drop into our house, we'd try to say a prayer, or do these games at the table, and it became apparent that we believed in Christ. Either we would initiate it or they would, or we would try to witness through our lives. One of my best friends was an agnostic, and I was able to witness to her, so that she came to the Lord and accepted him. We can share on that level. One boy that lived across the street from us was leading our son into drugs. I felt like Satan was trying to take dominion over our house, and I was constantly praying against it. And when we were about to move away, the children came home one day, and said that this young man had tooted his horn at them and said, 'I've been saved.' Later he came over and said, 'Mrs. Hogg, I was a Satan worshiper, and I prayed to cast spells on your house. But I want you to know that I've found Jesus, and you were instrumental in my being saved.' God was victorious over him; it was just tremendous!'"

Similarly, Bill has sought to make a Christian witness in his legal profession—especially through trying to apply his faith to the decisions he has to make. He describes it this way: "Christian ethics is a difficult thing to find. I'm the manager of patent operations in my company, and that company demands the highest ethical standards. So far I haven't had an occasion where the company has asked me to do anything that I would consider against my Christian ethics. I work within the framework of the Christian faith, and I will not compromise that understanding.

"But one of the struggles I have had in private law practice is when I was representing a client, and I had taken an oath to represent that client's interest to the best of my ability. Sometimes the causes were unpopular. When I was in private practice, one of the things I had to wrestle with as an attorney, and as a Christian, was if I was representing somebody I knew was guilty. When you're putting up a defense, how far can you go as a Christian? If you feel you can't go to a certain length as a Christian, yet your duty to that client suggests that you should go farther in representing the client, what do you do? When you are doing things that are getting out toward the limit—within the bounds of what the profession would consider ethical, but maybe stretching as to what a Christian should do, do you owe your client a duty? That's where the dilemma lies. You know that, if you push it to the limit, you may get your client off even though he or she is guilty. And if you don't, the client might sue you for malpractice. That's when the decisions get difficult for me as a Christian." Bill Hogg is seeking to be faithful as a Christian disciple in his practice of law, but not finding it easy.

Sustained Through Small Group Fellowship

Just as the Hoggs' adult Christian experience was inaugurated in small, intimate Christian groups (in Lay Witness Missions, a charismatic fellowship, and a Christian couples' club) so does their faith journey continue to be nurtured and sustained through small group fellowship. Marilyn participates in the Christian Women's Club, a nondenominational Bible study group. Together, they belong to a prayer-and-share group that meets twice a month. Wherever they have gone—and they have moved frequently through the years—they have started small fellowship groups and led Lay Witness Missions—an activity that stresses faith-sharing in small groups. And their own family has itself been a small group—witnessing to their peers, saying prayers at the table, and talking together about their religious beliefs, about Jesus and what he means in their lives. Of course, they have participated in the regular worship and study life of their congregation, but these small group experiences have made the difference between nominal church activity and a vital, witnessing faith.

Witness really is the keynote to the Hoggs' faith journey. As Bill puts it, "I think that our mission is to witness, to present Christ. When that happens, persons accept Christ, and they will change. To the extent that each of them changes and joins a community of believers, to that extent the world will change. We can't change anybody; all we can do is witness. God changes, we witness. And so to the extent that our witness creates a community, the world is transformed." Marilyn echoes Bill's words: "We can only witness. God is the one that saves, and we can only strive against Satan in our witness for God's power."

Bill and Marilyn Hogg are committed Christian disciples. Their faith journeys include childhood trauma and conversion, nominal participation growing into greater commitment, mutual influence toward deeper experience, small group acceptance and sharing, healings, family nurture, deliberate sharing of their faith, struggle with ethical issues, transformation through Lay Witness Missions, and witness—always witness—to their faith in Jesus Christ.

Questions for Thought and Discussion

1. The Hoggs were the only persons in this study who requested to be interviewed together. Is there faith experience similar enough to be described together, or have they been traveling on separate pathways?

2. What are the pros and cons of a shared religious experience for a

couple or family, as contrasted with an emphasis on each member cultivating his or her own individual spiritual life?

3. Bill and Marilyn lay heavy emphasis on the importance of Christian witness. What can you do to increase the capacity and opportunity for witnessing on the part of yourself and others in your church?

4. Compare and contrast your faith journey and those of your spouse and family with that of the Hoggs. What can you learn from their Christian experience that will help strengthen your marriage and family?

5. How can the small group ministry of your church be enhanced to better nurture the faith of your members?

6. How would you handle the ethical dilemma that Bill Hogg faced in his practice of law? What ethical decisions do you face in your life, and how does your faith throw light on these and help you know what to do?

4. ROBERT CROCKER: STRETCHING OUT IN FAITH

"I don't recall any time when I turned my back on my faith. Instead, I continue to search for more understanding. I feel confident that more will be revealed to me as I study and learn more about God. I now understand more because I have experienced more. I stretch out in faith." Robert Crocker, age thirty-nine, is just retired from the Navy and studying to go into real estate.

"I Felt Like Somebody Special"

Robert's faith journey began at age seven when he was baptized in a black Baptist church in the South. "It took place during a revival. I remember sitting on the mourner's bench, and I was baptized in a pool outside the church. My feeling was basically one of fear. The minister was very tall, and he had on high-water boots. He put his hand over my nose, submerged me in the water, and brought me back up. I felt like somebody special that day! I wore white. After the baptism, I changed my clothes and had a different place to sit in the church. This was the most memorable experience of my life."

The most formative influence in Robert's early life was his grand-mother. "My grandmother took me to church. We went to church and Sunday school and stayed all day. She was the mother of the church. It was so much a part of her life. It was not thought of as a separate occasion. She emphasized God's interactions in whatever happened—sickness, death, or any kind of trouble. One of her favor-ite sayings was, 'God expects more of us than this.' Whenever I was with grandmother, I was in church. I saw through her faith what faith could do. She was a living example."

The model of a faithful disciple who involved him in the church from the start became a guiding light in Robert's life. "I grew up in the Sunday school and church. They were always a part of my life. The true value of this I did not understand until I joined the Navy and left home. I carried a small Bible with me wherever I went, and while I was in the service I always went to church."

Religion was practiced at home as well. "Grace at meals was a big thing. She also made us pray before bed at night: 'Now I lay me down to sleep.' I lived with my grandmother in the summer and with my mother the rest of the time. My mother would sing spirituals while doing the laundry, with tears in her eyes. This memory is deep and abiding."

Persons close to him, who felt their faith deeply and were faithful to the church, had a powerful emotional influence on Robert, in devel-oping his religious habits and attitudes. "I felt that Christianity was something that people could feel, and in which they could find relief, joy, and confidence. They had a faith that whatever came about, it was not tied to other forces of the world, but was tied to a force that gave them faith and assurance."

This faith sustained Robert during a trying time in high school. "During my last year of high school, my mother was in the hospital, and I lived with different members of the family. I did a lot of thinking about Christianity. My grandmother asked me to keep God with me. I made it a point to go to church and Sunday school, even though the people I lived with did not. I experienced individual prayer and meditation. If anybody was on my side, God was." The example and guidance of his grandmother, and the church-going habits she had instilled in him, kept Robert related to the church and in touch with God even when external circumstances could well have discour-aged him.

"I Followed the Path in Which I Was Brought Up"

The influence of his mother, grandmother, and childhood church experiences stayed with Robert on into his adult life, particularly in his military career. "I went into the service at age eighteen, the day after graduating from high school. In the military I continued to go to church services. I followed the path I was brought up in.

"But some people in the service were not from a religious environment. This caused me to begin questioning. I examined the faith through several eyes. I found emptiness in people's lives who did not have faith." Robert went on to illustrate by telling of a submarine officer of his who was an atheist. When one of their mutual friends was killed in a car accident, the officer had nowhere to turn for consolation. So he attended the Christian memorial service in which Robert participated, and appeared to find comfort in this experience.

It was the advice and example of his grandmother that kept Robert faithful through his years in the Navy. "She told me to keep my Bible with me and read it, and that I would find comfort in it. I did get lonely, and I read my Bible often."

He did have his weak moments, though. "Sometimes I was not a strong Christian. I did go rabble-rousing with the other fellows." He was helped through this struggle by the opportunity to conduct services aboard the nuclear submarine to which he was assigned. "They needed someone to lead Sunday services. I volunteered. I prepared during the week. I talked to the chaplain before going to sea. They called me a lay leader. I presented a service more like a Bible study. That's where my Christian life took a real shot in the arm— from having to work on that."

Later Robert faced several crises which tested his faith. First, he "came down with a serious illness, and became fearful for my life. For several hours I was near death, but felt a close relationship with God. I prayed constantly that God would give me a chance—so I could be with my family, so my children could grow up as I wanted them to be. And God answered my prayer and allowed me to live, so I could have the influence on their lives that they needed."

On another occasion Robert faced a court battle for custody of his children, whom he felt better qualified to care for than his former wife. "I had responsibility for two children from my previous marriage. I prayed that God would help me guide their growth. One night in the barracks I prayed. I didn't know what to do. I wanted to do right by them. This gave me courage to go to court and ask for custody. Through meditation I came to the conclusion that this was what I should do. I felt God wanted me to take care of my kids, so I went to court and fought for custody."

A third crisis came when Robert was called upon to fire a missile. He was afraid that it might blow up his submarine, and also was concerned about the lives it might take upon impact. "This required me to rely on my faith. I prayed and thanked God for the life I had had so far, and asked, if I was worthy, to please accept me into God's kingdom. I turned it all over to God. There I was, two or three hundred feet under water, and I could feel God's presence. I could seek and pray even when I couldn't go to church. So I know from this experience that there's nothing else like Christianity. You can always have God with you. You can turn to God."

Through all his twenty years in the Navy, Robert was sustained by memories of his childhood church experience, the guiding advice and example of his grandmother, continued church-going whenever possible, and reliance on prayer and Bible reading in times of loneliness, temptation, and crisis.

"I Decided to Join the Church"

After retiring from the Navy, Robert moved to a large Southern city to prepare for a career in real estate. "Prior to that I had not made a commitment because I was out at sea for three months at a time. I started attending a Primitive Baptist church, and then I decided to join the church. My wife wasn't ready, but when I joined she did too. Now she is stronger in the faith than I am. Our family has gained. We are a family in the church. I wanted an opportunity to serve God, and there are many in this church. It is rewarding to teach Sunday school. The church has retreats, and in these I see myself grow. I have grown to see that Christianity has contributed much to making me who I am." Robert was led back into the church both for what it would do for him and also so he could render service to others.

His was a searching faith, though. He had lots of questions. "I always questioned Christianity and faith, was always looking to see what Christianity offered me. I wondered about those who were not Christian: Where do they find faith? As a young person I didn't understand what was in the Bible; I was confused; I felt that I should believe everything. I asked about the Passover: 'Why would God kill all those children?' I didn't understand; it was a blockage. I had to have reasons for everything. But then I came to realize that I didn't have to understand it all. God was not revealing it all to me right now. So, I'm going to do what I think God wants me to do. That's when it turns out right. I know this works. So I can tell my Sunday school class: 'Have faith in God, and serving God will pay off.'"

"My Motives Are to Do What Is Christian"

Robert does not have all the answers by any means, but his continuing search and his life in the church give him the stability and sense of direction to carry on in his journey of discipleship. "Christianity does it for me. I sometimes feel tempted to do what human beings think is right. But I am able to conquer peer pressure because my motives are to do what is Christian. I examine what I am doing in a Christian vein. I don't do foolish things. As a Christian I have a responsibility to live a sensible life. God calls us to be disciples, to be out in the world and to show them what Christianity can do. I try to show that it's all right to be a Christian. Christianity is a joyous thing—a good way to live. In real estate you can have Christian principles in everything you do. Just do the Christian thing. What has gotten me this far on the journey is just being a Christian." Sustained by the church and his Christian heritage, Robert seeks to express his faith in every arena of his life.

He continues to have his struggles, though—both in understanding and interpreting some of the mysteries of life, and also in relating his faith to global issues. "Death is one thing I struggle with. Just last week the father of one of my Sunday school students was killed accidentally. I searched and prayed for understanding, in order to be supportive to her. I helped her see that God takes the pain away. We gain from loving those close to us. The pain of loss of loved ones is the price we pay for loving them."

Robert also strives to understand and relate to the big issues in the world. "That's the area I'm weakest in—relating Christianity and faith in God to those issues. What's happening there is sinful—war, corruption, the nuclear arms race, murder, molesting children. I wonder why these things happen. It must be because some people's faith is weak. I want to do something about them, but don't know what to do. The only thing I know to do is pray about these tragedies. I have a lot of compassion. A lot of things concern me—things that cause human pain. I wish they didn't have that pain. In due time, God will rule in all these matters. This too will pass. In God's own time these things will have an answer and a resolution."

Through times of loneliness, fear, doubt, rabble-rousing, personal crisis, separation from family, and life transition, Robert Crocker has been sustained in his faith by memory, prayer, relationship, conscience, and a sense of direction. There have been lapses, questions, and struggles, but he has stayed with the church, found avenues of service, maintained his relationship with God, kept on growing, and continues to be nurtured and sustained in the faith community.

Questions for Thought and Discussion

1. At what points in Robert's life do you see God at work in special ways?

2. How has the church fostered Robert's growth in faith and discipleship? What can you and your church learn from his experience in the church?

3. What are the similarities and differences between Robert's faith journey and yours? How could the sharing of your faith story challenge others to grow as his does?

4. What biblical stories, themes, or verses are you reminded of by Robert's story?

5. What is your response to Robert's questions about death, the reason behind social problems and tragedies, and not understanding some things in the Bible?

6. What do you think about his statement, "Have faith in God, and serving God will pay off"?

CHAPTER FOUR

MINISTRIES ENABLING FAITH AND COMMITMENT

What can we learn from the faith stories in this book about how we can share our faith experiences in ways that encourage one another to grow in faith and discipleship? How can we become better able to tell others how we are becoming Christian? How can congregations make the task of helping persons become Christian central to their life and ministry?

For all the persons who have told their stories in this book, the church has played a significant role in leading them to Christ, nurturing their growth in faith and leading them to express their commitment in a life of discipleship and service. All were asked the question, "How has the church assisted you in your faith journey, or how do you wish it had?" Most were also asked to describe what a congregation would look like that was giving priority in its program to fostering members' growth in faith and discipleship. In addition, the stories of these persons suggest ways for us to help other persons make a step of faith that moves them along in their journey.

These approaches to ministry fall into three categories—personal ministries by and to individuals, church plans and programs, and outreach beyond the congregation into the community and world. We will examine each of these in turn.

A. Personal Ministries

Four types of individual strategies can be described. For some, a person serving as a model or example of the Christian life or faith was the key factor in leading them to deeper commitment. For others, it was the influence of a family member or the faith practiced by the family as a whole. Others pointed to a personal relationship through which they were led to deeper faith. A fourth group identified the intentional cultivation of their growth in faith by a pastor or other interested person as the primary influence in their lives at a critical time.

1. MODELS OF FAITH

For a number of persons in the study, the example of another, often a pastor, was an important influence in their faith journey. The witness of a caring, committed life makes a powerful impression, sometimes without the knowledge of the model him- or herself.

One man remarked that, as he was growing up, it was his pastor's sermons that impressed him. His knowledge of the Bible and ability to prepare and organize his thoughts on a weekly basis captured this boy's interest and prompted him to explore the faith in greater depth as he grew older.

For one woman, it was the trust, love, and acceptance of the pastor of her youth that had a profound influence. It gave her much-needed affirmation and became for her a reminder of the constant presence of God in her life.

Another woman cited the example of a caring pastor who preached direct sermons, built the congregation into a close community, and took a personal interest in individual members. These qualities led her to get more involved in the church and take her faith more seriously. This same woman was influenced by the example of her mother, whose faith and pluck after the death of her father enabled her whole family to survive a very difficult period in their lives.

One young man took his inspiration from the Roman Catholic priest who was his high school teacher and advisor, and, as friend and counselor, "was the man who showed me the gospel." This person was also profoundly influenced by the example of several lay persons—a Sunday school teacher who knelt and prayed with him in an effort to lead him to Christ, and the people in his new church home who expressed kindness, patience, and understanding toward him.

These and other instances show that the modeling of faith by competent, caring, and intentional Christians—both pastors and laity—does make a significant impact on the faith of others. Attitudes of diligence, faithful witness, friendly concern, hopefulness, and affirmation of the gifts of others, will bear fruit in unexpected ways as persons imitate and explore the faith of those they admire and appreciate. Frequent reminders of the importance of example, training in the skills of caring, and emphasis on the incarnational nature of Christian faith—God's love embodied in human lives—all will contribute to a congregational strategy of growing faith through personal example.

2. FAITH IN FAMILIES

For some persons the family is the primary environment that nurtures faith. One man remembered regular grace at meals as a formative influence. A woman recalled the songs about Jesus her mother used to sing. Another yearned to have "a Christian family where we actually say grace, light Advent candles, and do a little worship," realizing that what she had missed in her own childhood home would be important for her baby son to experience as he grew up. She saw the significance of husband and wife sharing a common faith perspective and commitment in order to provide a consistent nurturing environment for fostering faith in their children.

One couple made their home a center of Christian witness to neighbors and friends of their children. Their mealtime prayers in the presence of guests, and sharing their faith with troubled teenagers brought home by their kids, were reminders "that we believed in God" and contributed to leading some persons to Christ.

These examples point to the central importance of the family in shaping the faith of children, supporting the growth and witness of spouses, and making the home a center of Christian discipleship that touches the lives of others as well. The church can provide encouragement, guidance, and training to enable family groupings to fulfill this role.

3. PERSONAL RELATIONSHIPS

Perhaps the most frequently cited factor in leading persons to deeper awareness and greater commitment in their faith journeys was the influence of another person in the context of a meaningful relationship.

A grandmother, who was "the mother of the church" and had a vital relationship with God, gave one man a Bible when he joined the Navy, and was the major reason he continued going to church all the time he was in the service.

For another woman, it was a school teacher aunt who "believed in the Lord with all her heart and soul," came home on weekends to read the Bible to her, and gave her an example of living one's beliefs. Since their marriage, this woman and her husband have influenced each other's growth in faith through family devotions, mutual encouragement, and active sharing together in the life of the church.

A young adult mentioned the strict moral upbringing of his parents and the regular church and Sunday school attendance of his boyhood friends, in addition to the Sunday school teacher who prayed with him, as important influences in his faith journey. For another young man, it was the insistence of his fiancée that he become a Christian before she would marry him that started him on the road to Christian discipleship. Another man was touched by the personal warmth of a Bible professor in college, even though he does not remember much of the content of his courses.

A young woman was befriended at a bus stop by a Roman Catholic woman who shared her faith and invited her to a home Bible study. For another young woman, it was the church secretary who became her best friend, to whom she could tell her problems, and from whom she could gain understanding and support as she sought to apply her newfound faith to a troubled home situation.

For all these persons, a close relationship with one or more persons of faith was a key factor that moved them along in their own faith journeys. They were either led to make a personal commitment to Jesus Christ or were influenced in that direction by a relative or friend who took the time and interest to share faith and love with them. You can be outgoing in sharing your faith by word and deed in these and other ways, and also can be intentional about introducing a faith dimension into your personal and family relationships.

4. CULTIVATION OF INDIVIDUAL GROWTH

Some pastors in congregations make a special point to identify the needs and gifts of individual members and then to cultivate their growth in faith along these lines.

A sensitive pastor invited one woman to teach confirmation, an experience that challenged and enriched her and gave her a sense of being in ministry. Later, when she was approaching burnout, her pastor and congregation gave her time off to reflect and recoup her energies—again in response to her need at that point in her spiritual journey.

Just out of the Navy, one man was only twenty-two when approached by an alert pastor to chair his church's every member canvass. Sensing his eagerness and abilities in the financial area, this man's pastor launched him into a form of lay ministry that has developed over the years and led him deeper and deeper into a committed and imaginative faith. He is now involved in his present congregation in encouraging and supporting the development of the gifts of other laity for their ministries in the world.

After her new birth experience, one young woman was struggling with making a complete surrender of herself to Christ and also with a vocational choice. A supportive pastor helped her make both important decisions.

Several of those interviewed reported that they had been guided in reading the Bible and other books by a sensitive pastor and/or a supportive sharing or study group. Some had been given a particular book to read at a time when it spoke meaningfully to a specific need or question they were facing, and thereby contributed to a significant deepening in faith and discipleship.

A Japanese-American woman told of a pastor who got her active in the church, another pastor and wife who made many visits to their home and "finally succeeded . . . in getting my husband to accept Christ and become a Christian," and also a United Methodist Women's unit that elected her to office and then said, "We'll help you" to learn and perform her job.

In these and other ways, pastors and congregations can pay attention to where individual members are in their faith journeys; offer resources, opportunities, and suggestions for enabling growth; and provide individual guidance and support for the personal faith struggles and openings that people are facing.

B. The Life of the Church

A second type of ministry approach contributing to growth in faith is the area of congregational life and program. The general climate or ethos of a congregation can contribute to developing faith and commitment. The worship services, programming, and facilities also can be structured to contribute to this end. Teaching and training events can be organized with a focus on the faith of both teachers and learners. Small groups of various types are an especially effective means of sharing and nurturing faith. And the provision of service opportunities also gives impetus to deeper commitment in discipleship.

1. Congregational Ethos

The general atmosphere in a congregation may be more or less conducive to growth in faith. One young man, after visiting several churches in his quest for a church home, commented with great appreciation on the open, free, friendly, caring climate he found in the Lutheran church he eventually decided to join. His faith was challenged and nurtured by the warmth, acceptance, lack of pressure, and absence of cliques in this congregation.

A young woman expressed her appreciation for the pluralistic, accepting nature of the United Methodist church with which she chose to unite. She found in this congregation "my Christian family," and experienced among these people an openness to diversity and a spiritual warmth that both challenged and supported her search, and left her free to think, struggle, and explore in her own individual way.

Another woman pointed to the opportunity provided by her church to engage in activities that developed her abilities and gave expression to her budding faith. She also appreciated their welcoming attitude toward immigrants and newcomers, the continuity of lay leadership during times of pastoral change, and the stability fostered by long-term pastorates. These qualities of church life made it possible for her to be understood, supported, and challenged in her faith journey by both pastoral and lay leaders.

These and similar elements contribute to the ethos of a congregation that is deliberate and effective in fostering growth in faith. An ethos is intangible and sometimes difficult to change, but a congregation must be aware of its internal climate and its effect on persons, and seek to make it as encouraging as possible to growth in faith.

2. Worship Services

As might be expected, the nature and quality of the worship service is an important factor in cultivating personal faith. Two men mentioned participation in worship while serving in the armed forces as being a significant influence during that crucial stage in their lives. One also credited the all-student church in which he worshiped during college as helping to shape his beliefs and values. A young woman was nourished by going every Sunday to "celebrate, praise God, and express my faith."

In addition to these general positive influences, specific aspects of the worship service or particular types of worship were also mentioned by some as having special meaning. One young man was powerfully influenced by the service in which he was baptized and confirmed. He also appreciated the symbolism of the sanctuary and sacraments, especially Holy Communion. The charismatic meeting he attended for awhile, characterized as it was by lively singing, intense sincerity, and "praising God with your whole spirit," became for a time a "a really exciting form of Christian worship" for him.

A young woman liked the didactic sermons of the pastor in her new church, because she was in need of basic teaching in order to ground and feed her rapidly growing faith. Others responded positively to testimonials, an altar call, and a healing service at important stages in their journeys.

What is clearly implied in these comments is that different elements in worship appeal to different people at different times in their lives— according to their past experiences and needs of the moment. Both formal and informal worship experiences, and both evangelistic and instructional preaching, are appropriate and needed by persons in most congregations.

3. Teaching and Training Opportunities

Many of the persons interviewed in the study cited educational experiences in the church as playing a vital role in their growth in faith and discipleship. Confirmation and adult membership classes, Bible training and memorization as a child, good church school teaching, and studies and classes on human rights and peace and justice, were among the specific types of teaching and training mentioned.

Parochial school experiences, characterized by caring teachers, stimulating religious instruction, and the overall Christian ethos of the school, were important catalysts to religious growth for a few. Experience in college religion classes and Conference Schools of Christian Mission expanded and deepened faith perspectives for several.

One young woman expressed a strong need for substance and answers in her religious education even as a child, a need which did not get met for her until her adult years. Perhaps this is reflective of the experience of others as well—persons who either consciously or unconsciously are searching for a religious foundation for their lives.

4. Church Programs and Facilities

In addition to teaching and training experiences that contributed to faith development, other church programs mentioned by persons in the study included Lay Witness Missions, revival meetings, evangelistic crusades, and forums on contemporary social issues.

The use of church facilities can also be planned with a view to attracting people and introducing them to the faith dimension of life. Two examples of this in the current project were the after-school study done in the church by a high school girl, and the church center for young adults and service personnel where one person met his wife.

A key guideline in determining church programming and use of facilities must be their contribution to nurturing the faith of those involved. Programs of an evangelistic nature that attract persons to the church and introduce them to Jesus Christ can be balanced with others that challenge them to grow deeper and expand their faith horizons.

5. Small Groups

A particular type of programming that is especially conducive to sharing and nurturing faith is the small group. A variety of small group experiences were reported by persons as making a significant impact on their faith journeys. Church youth groups, Bible study groups, a church basketball team, Christian couples' clubs, Sunday school classes, prayer and share groups, charismatic fellowships, Christian women's clubs, home study groups, an interdenominational high school prayer group, lay ministry support groups, campus Christian groups—these and other small groups were all found meaningful and influential by persons interviewed in nurturing their growth in faith and discipleship.

Small groups provide a context for intimate sharing of personal faith experiences, mutual support and acceptance, deepening through prayer and study, and challenge to a more intentional living out of one's discipleship. The congregation interested in focusing on growth in faith will provide a variety of small group experiences for its members.

6. Service Opportunities

A balanced faith must move beyond a private, inner experience to expression in service to others. The persons interviewed in this project described a variety of service opportunities provided by the church that challenged them to grow by giving themselves for others.

Several found in teaching Sunday school a stimulus to developing their own knowledge and commitment. Another gained special satisfaction through teaching confirmation. Others had held a variety of positions in the church, including committee chairperson, stewardship drive director, women's society officer, lay speaker, and chaplain's assistant. Such opportunities both enable persons to grow in their ability to develop and express their own faith and at the same time resource the faith of others.

One businessman, in his faith journey, moved steadily from traditional forms of service in the congregation to prophetic and risky witness as a change agent, and in the process developed deeper biblical and theological understanding and greater commitment to Christ.

The ministry of the laity takes a variety of forms, each of which provides opportunity both for growth in and expression of one's faith. The faith-focused congregation will be intentional about so structuring its life as to involve laity in service and witness to Christ, the church, and world, as a means to both formation and expression of faith and discipleship.

C. Congregational Outreach

Related to the Christian service of individuals is the missional orientation of the whole congregation toward meeting the needs of others. Such a priority serves to raise the commitment of members to both evangelistic witness and social concern, as well as to address society and individuals outside the church with the redemptive promise and power of Jesus Christ. Four types of outreach that foster growth in faith and discipleship were identified: pastoral care of persons with problems, proclamation through the media, evangelistic witness, and social concern.

1. Pastoral Care

Persons facing problems tend to be preoccupied by them and thus unable to hear and respond to the message of the gospel until they get help. Pastoral care provided by the church thus is not only a service offering the love of Christ to hurting persons, but also may prepare them for hearing and accepting the Word of God at deeper levels.

Examples of this care were the intentional ministry to people in transition of one woman's congregation, and the need for ministry to immigrant youth and to children of divorce evidenced in another woman's story. These and other instances demonstrate the church's caring ministry, expressed unreservedly to all persons, and can become the means by which some are launched or assisted in their faith journeys. The experience of providing pastoral care to others also contributes to a growing faith for the helper.

2. Media Proclamation

Some persons interviewed mentioned books such as *Karen* and films such as *Jesus Christ, Superstar* as making a significant contribution to their growth in faith and discipleship. Magazines, television and radio, and audio and video cassettes represent other avenues for communicating the gospel. The media approach, so characteristic of life in the late twentieth century, can be an effective means for churches to communicate the gospel and nurture faith and commitment.

3. Evangelistic Witness

Outreach to persons finds its premiere expression in the personal witness seeking to lead others to make a commitment of faith in Jesus Christ. Examples of this include the evangelical witness of youth peers in high school and college, and the influence on a Buddhist young adult of a devout Chinese couple he lived with in Hawaii.

The importance of a positive, sensitive witness is illustrated by the experience of one woman's uncle, who lived with a strong Christian family who attempted to force their Bible and faith on others to the point that "he just began to despise the Christian religion," and later would not allow her to attend church during the years she was staying with him. Evangelistic witness must be outspoken and courageous, of course, but not at the cost of turning people off through overzealous, aggressive efforts at conversion.

Several of those interviewed also expressed a strong desire to share their faith with others through personal witnessing. One couple had devoted considerable time and energy over the years to informal witnessing to friends and neighbors, and also to structured witnessing through Lay Witness Missions in local churches. Another young woman indicated significant interest in leading her agnostic husband into the same meaningful experience with Christ that she had found. One person put it this way: "I now want to reach out to other members of the church who are not active, and persons outside the church, and witness or share my faith with them."

There is something about vital Christian faith that demands to be shared with others. Congregations oriented to equipping people for the faith journey will give priority to challenging and training persons to give verbal expression to their faith in ways that lead others to meet and follow Jesus Christ.

4. Social Concern

Living faith also inevitably seeks expression in all of life, striving to impact the world and bring it into harmony with the just and loving purpose of God. Probably the best example of this was a man who sought to apply his faith to the areas of finance and stewardship, racism and sexism, and justice and fairness in his business world. Similarly, a lawyer expressed a strong desire to relate Christian values to his defense of clients; a black realtor sought to express his faith in the way he conducted his business; a woman saw the relevance of her Christian commitment to women's liberation issues; a grandfather was motivated by his faith to engage in the gay rights movement; and a civilian educator was concerned to apply his Christian convictions in the way he carried out education programs in the Air Force.

One young man saw immediate relevance of his growing faith to the racial prejudice against blacks seeking to move into his neighborhood. A Japanese-American woman was involved with her congregation in peace activism and in ministry to new immigrants from Japan and to the homeless beach people in Honolulu. A New Zealand Methodist layman was working to build understanding and reconciliation between the white majority and the Maori people in his homeland.

One young woman, who had been turned off by her parents' social activism without a theological base, and who for the present preferred to devote her energies to more inward and congregational expressions of faith, still appreciated the social concern of other members of her new congregation, saying, "I'm glad that people are socially active here."

Service to the needy, protest against social injustice, efforts toward peace and reconciliation, and action in cooperation with God to transform a sinful world into a more fitting expression of the biblical vision of shalom, are all avenues for the expression of faith and discipleship which challenge persons to greater Christian commitment.

It is evident from this overview that persons who are "becoming Christian," through whatever pathway, need churches that invite them, personally and directly, to accept Jesus Christ as Savior and

Lord. They need churches that prepare them to respond to this challenge by teaching them the biblical story, by fostering their personal relationship with God through prayer and worship, by providing concern and support during times of personal crisis and transition, and by setting examples of faithful Christian living and witnessing. They need churches in which people sensitively but unashamedly share their faith journey with one another—in personal conversation, small support groups, and public meetings. They need churches that challenge persons to deeds of discipleship in service of persons who are in need. These persons need churches which will protest against social injustice and act to bring about systemic change.

In short, for persons to become Christian, churches are needed that make the discipling of persons in the Christian faith their central purpose—undergirding and giving focus to everything they do.

Questions for Thought and Discussion

1. How has your church helped you in your faith journey, or how do you wish it had?

2. Describe what a congregation would look like that was giving priority in its program to fostering growth in faith and discipleship among its members.

3. Which of the approaches to ministry described in this chapter have been helpful to you personally? What has made them so? Which of them will be most useful to your congregation? How will you seek to implement them?

4. What faith-focused ministry strategies, not mentioned in this chapter, have been personally helpful to you, or might be relevant and meaningful to your congregation or constituency?

5. What is your response to the conclusion of this chapter that, for persons to become Christian, churches are needed that make the discipling of persons in the Christian faith the central focus of all they do?

6. Sit down and write out your faith story in a form that could be shared with a person or group in order to stimulate them to take the invitation of Jesus Christ more seriously.

CHAPTER FIVE

SHARING YOUR
FAITH STORY

How have you become Christian? How has the church helped in this process, or how do you wish it had? How do you feel about sharing your faith story with other persons in your church? With members of your family? With friends and co-workers? With strangers? Here are some practical suggestions to help you share your faith journey with others in ways that invite them to think more deeply about their relationship with God and God's purpose for their lives.

1. *Reflect on your own story.* Keep a journal in which you record significant experiences in the past and present, and your thoughts and feelings about them. Describe the event and then reflect on such questions as these: What is God doing and saying to me in this experience? How am I becoming Christian through this process? What factors or influences have helped me grow in faith and discipleship? What part have other Christians and the church played? How am I cooperating with or resisting the movement of God's Spirit in my life? What growth is still needed in this area of my life?

2. *Ground yourself in scripture.* Read the Bible devotionally every day. Study the historical and literary background of the book and chapter you are reading through use of a good commentary. Look for major themes and the primary thrust of each passage. Relate the biblical story to your own faith story by trying to identify parallels and crossing points. Ask, How is my story like that of Daniel, Ruth, Moses, or Esther? Where in my life are things going on like what happened with Peter, Mary, Timothy, or Lydia? In what ways might I

be wandering in the desert, trying to sing the Lord's song in a strange land, or coming to myself and returning to God? What is my burning bush? Am I the shallow soil or the good soil? Is my house built on the sand or the rock? Have I put my light under a bushel or on a lampstand? Who am I in the light of scripture?

3. *Listen carefully to those with whom you share.* Be sensitive to their expressions of interest and need. Familiarize yourself with their life situation. Keep good eye contact, observe their response, and watch for points of contact. Hear and respond to their feelings as well as their ideas. Reframe their comments and feelings, paraphrasing what they say so they know they are really heard. Relate the telling of your story to relevant aspects of their experience. Identify with them at their point of pain, doubt, or struggle, and share your own journey as it relates to those points. Hear them out, fully and deeply, and do not force your story on them. Wait until they are ready and willing, even eager, to hear you.

4. *Pray and seek God's guidance.* Practicing sensitivity to God's Spirit will make you sensitive to the other. Ask God to help you "listen with the third ear," that is, with a heart of understanding and com-passion (feeling with). Pray for guidance on when and how and what of your story to share. Pray silently before, during, and after the conversation. Beforehand, pray that God will make the person open and receptive, and that your sharing will be respectful of the person and relevant to his or her need. During the conversation, ask for sensitivity to hear accurately and wisdom to respond aright. Afterwards, pray that the Spirit will continue to work in the person's heart and that the seeds you have sown may take root and grow.

5. *Share your story as your personal experience, not as a formula which the other must follow.* Explain that this is what you believe God has been doing in your life, and that it is up to the other to try to discern what God may be saying and doing with her or him. Show the parallels between your story and the biblical story, and stress that, while the crossing points may be different for another person, serious searching will surely discover them in illuminating and life-changing ways. Emphasize that God loves each person, respects our freedom, and seeks us each in our own unique way. Tell your story simply and

directly, and then leave the other free to respond as she or he wills. Do not press for a particular kind of response, but make yourself available—now or later—to be present, listen, and be supportive.

6. *Invite the other to be a companion with you on the journey.* Do not expect the one conversation to be all there is to this relationship. To share faith stories is to begin a journey together. Invite the person to be with you in the worship and fellowship life of the church. Join a sharing, prayer, or support group together. Offer to be present with him or her in ongoing conversation, frank dialogue, shared struggle, and honest search. Suggest or loan books that have been meaningful to you. Share scripture passages that have thrown light on your life. Go to movies, follow the news, or watch TV or videos together, and then discuss the faith issues that emerge. Tell more of your story, and in more depth, as your relationship grows and the occasion calls for it. Be available to make the other person part of your story, and yourself part of his/hers.

7. *Begin by sharing your faith story with fellow Christians in the church.* Form a faith-sharing group and meet regularly for prayer, Bible study, and personal storytelling. Either take turns sharing your entire spiritual autobiographies week by week, or else in a given meeting have each member share single incidents related to a particular theme. For example, persons could tell their prodigal son experiences, their Damascus Road experiences, their healings, examples of alienation and reconciliation, or how sin and grace have been expressed in their lives. Pray for one another in the meeting and during the week between meetings. Study together the biblical stories of persons of faith—such as Abraham and Sarah, Miriam and Moses, Ruth and Naomi, David and Jonathan, Peter and John, Priscilla and Aquila, Amos, Hosea, Isaiah, Jeremiah, Daniel, and Stephen. Look for and discuss the parallels between their lives and yours.

8. *Make this into a support group for your faith-sharing outside the church.* When you feel ready, challenge each other in the group to share your faith stories with one person outside the church each week. Devote a portion of each meeting to hearing reports of these encounters. Respond to members' accounts with sensitivity to feelings, encouragement of these outreach efforts, and suggestions for

follow-up. Urge members to record these conversations in their journals, and reflect on the feelings and themes that emerge, so they can more fully and accurately share them with the group. Provide both support and accountability for regular, prayerful, sensitive sharing of faith stories both in the church and in the world.

From the stories in this book, we have learned that persons develop in faith and discipleship in basically two ways—individually or communally. Persons who are awakened to faith personally become Christian through experiences of crisis or turmoil, the stimulus of a significant relationship, the pursuit of a religious quest, or the process of gradual maturing in faith. Those whose faith experience is integrally related to the church become Christian through the nurture of the faith community, the challenge of service and social action, the stable, steady life of discipleship, or involvement in small intimate groups.

Whether their experience is primarily individual or corporate, all are assisted in their faith journey by the ministries of the church. These are of three types.

Personal ministries include individuals who serve as models of faith, family expressions of faith, nurturing of faith in close personal relationships, and intentional cultivation of spiritual growth.

Ministries through **the life and program of the church** take the shape of formative congregational ethos, meaningful worship experiences, teaching and training opportunities, faith-focused church programs and use of facilities, faith-oriented small group experiences, and challenges to express faith and discipleship through service.

Congregational outreach that fosters faith includes pastoral care with persons in need, proclamation of the Christian message through the media, personal evangelistic witness, and involvement in social concern and action.

Persons who are becoming Christian need direct, personal invitations, and churches that make the discipling of persons in the Christian faith their central focus.

Personal faith-sharing must be based on reflection on one's own faith journey, biblical foundations and themes, careful listening to the other, a prayerful quest for God's guidance, respect not imposition, and an offer to be a companion on the journey. A faith-sharing group in the church can both nurture growth in faith and discipleship for members and also provide support and accountability for sharing one's story with persons outside the church.

What will you do with this call to reflect on and share your faith story? What is the current state of your personal faith journey? Which of the pathways to faith described in this book are familiar to you and which need further exploration? Which of the stories can you learn from as you seek to become more Christian yourself? How can you let the stories of faith told here become an impetus to share your story with others?

The journey of faith never ends. We never become fully Christian. There is always new growth, deeper commitment, more faithful discipleship lying ahead of us. Where will your faith journey take you next? What is God calling you to be and do as a result of reading this book? How and with whom will you tell your story of developing faith and discipleship?

And what about your church? What are you doing to help persons become Christian? How well do you and other members cultivate faith through example, relationships, family life, and intentional invitation, encouragement, and care? How would you evaluate the ethos of your congregation and each aspect of its program in terms of its contribution to calling and helping persons become Christian? To what extent are decisions about budget, facilities, and program made with a view to this central purpose? How intentional are you about encouraging persons to share their faith stories with one another and with persons outside the church? Do you have groups or other opportunities for nurture, training, support, and accountability for faith-sharing?

And, finally, what about your own Christian witness? How can you offer your faith story to others to assist their growth in faith and discipleship? How can you become more sensitive to the spiritual needs of others, more aware of the parallels between personal stories and the biblical story, more confident about sharing your religious experience and resources with others, and more firm about living out your beliefs through service and social concern? How can you become more intentional and skillful in sharing your faith story with others and becoming their companion on the journey of Christian faith?

Jesus told a parable about faith: "The kingdom of heaven is like a grain of mustard seed which a man took and sowed in his field; it is the smallest of all seeds, but when it has grown it is the greatest of shrubs and becomes a tree, so that the birds of the air come and make nests in its branches" (Matthew 13:31-32).

This is the nature of faith. It starts small and can grow large. It requires sowing, cultivation, and care. It multiplies its effects. It provides hospitality for other creatures.

The people who have shared their faith with us in this book illustrate this. The seed of faith has been sown in their lives in a variety of ways. The seed has been nurtured by themselves and others in homes, groups, and churches. It has grown large in its impact on their lives, families, churches, and communities— and also on us. It has provided hospitality for others in need or in search of acceptance and meaning, and faith has been multiplied as a result.

What is happening to the mustard seed that has taken root in you? How are you nurturing its growth and sharing its impact? How can you become more intentional about sowing these seeds in the hearts and lives of those about you? What is your church doing to cultivate the seeds of faith sown in their garden? Let your encounter with the faith stories in this book be the means of fostering new growth in faith and discipleship in you and in your congregation.